Studies in Natural Language Processing

Systemic text generation as problem solving

Studies in Natural Language Processing
Executive Editor: Aravind K. Joshi
Sponsored by the Association for Computational Linguistics

This series publishes monographs, texts, and edited volumes within the interdisciplinary field of computational linguistics. Sponsored by the Association for Computational Linguistics, the series represents the range of topics of concern to the scholars working in this increasingly important field, whether their background is in formal linguistics, psycholinguistics, cognitive psychology or artificial intelligence.

Also in this series:

Memory and context for language interpretation by Hiyan Alshawi
Planning English sentences by Douglas E. Appelt
Computational linguistics by Ralph Grishman
Language and spatial cognition by Annette Herskovits
Semantic interpretation and the resolution of ambiguity by Graeme Hirst
Text generation by Kathleen R. McKeown
Machine translation edited by Sergei Nirenburg
Machine translation systems edited by Jonathan Slocum

Systemic text generation as problem solving

TERRY PATTEN

Department of Computer and Information Science,
The Ohio State University

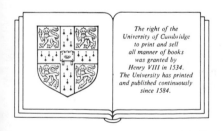

The right of the
University of Cambridge
to print and sell
all manner of books
was granted by
Henry VIII in 1534.
The University has printed
and published continuously
since 1584.

CAMBRIDGE UNIVERSITY PRESS

CAMBRIDGE

NEW YORK   NEW ROCHELLE

MELBOURNE   SYDNEY

Published by the Press Syndicate of the University of Cambridge
The Pitt Building, Trumpington Street, Cambridge CB2 1RP
32 East 57th Street, New York, NY 10022, USA
10 Stamford Road, Oakleigh, Melbourne 3166, Australia

© Cambridge University Press 1988

First published 1988

Printed in Great Britain at the University Press, Cambridge

ISBN 0 521 35076 X

325017

Contents

Contents

Contents

Contents

For my parents

Preface

The research reported here was done within the Department of Artificial Intelligence at the University of Edinburgh. All the chapters but one are, with some modifications, chapters from my doctoral thesis. The exception (Chapter 5), is a slightly revised version of a paper written jointly with Graeme Ritchie, that was presented at the Third International Workshop on Natural Language Generation.

I would like to thank my thesis supervisor, Graeme Ritchie, for his patient and constructive criticism throughout the development of this work, and of course, for his direct contribution to Chapter 5. My other supervisor, Austin Tate, and the rest of the Edinburgh planning group provided insights into AI problem solving. I would also like to thank my thesis examiners, C. S. Mellish and Henry Thompson, for their helpful suggestions. I am also grateful to Mark Drummond, Andy Golding and Chris Sothcott for valuable technical discussions, to Mark Kingwell for proof-reading the thesis draft, and to Aravind Joshi as editor of the Cambridge University Press *Studies in Natural Language Processing* series.

This research was supported in part by Alberta and Canada Student Loans, and an Overseas Research Student Award. The word-processing and typesetting facilities used in the preparation of the final draft were kindly provided by the Department of Computer Science at the University of Calgary.

1
Introduction

This book explores a new approach to text generation that interprets systemic grammar as a computational representation. Systemic grammars are interpreted as domain-specific knowledge and used by an artificial intelligence problem solver to solve text-generation problems. This is made possible by a fundamental, but hitherto unrecognized, relationship between systemic grammar and problem solving. This approach solves the methodological problem of interfacing specialized knowledge-based computational representations with equally specialized linguistic representations—because in this case the representation is the same. Previously, text-generation systems have had to make either linguistic sacrifices for computational reasons or computational sacrifices for linguistic reasons.

This approach to text generation has been investigated through two different channels. The primary means of investigation has been a substantial implementation involving a relatively large systemic grammar. The secondary means of investigation has been the construction of a formal model. Aside from a detailed discussion of the approach to text generation, the implementation, and the formal model, the topics covered in this book include the relevant background in artificial intelligence (AI) problem solving and systemic grammar, a comparison with other work in the field, and a sampling of ideas for future research.

1.1. The scientific context

Work in the area of natural-language processing has appeared under several banners, each of which has associated objectives and assumptions. It is therefore important to clarify the objectives and assumptions of the present work. Perhaps it would be best to begin by explicitly stating some of the fields of study to which *no* contribution has been intended.

Some of the work in natural-language processing, and in particular text generation, is intended to have psychological implications (e.g. McDonald, 1980). No such implications are intended here. It is hoped that, like any other AI research, this work may provide useful suggestions and concepts for future psychological description (see Ritchie, 1980, p.19).

Some other work in natural-language processing is intended to introduce or develop a linguistic theory (e.g. ibid.). Although the theory of systemic grammar is central to this work, no attempt has been made, with the exception of some formalization, to contribute to the existing theory. This point must be emphasized since one of the most important claims that *is* made here is that an established linguistic theory has been used and has not been tampered with in any way.

Finally, although the state-of-the-art AI problem-solving techniques play a central role in this work, no attempt has been made to advance this state-of-the-art. This too must be emphasized since the credibility of this approach to text generation depends on the use of indubitable problem-solving techniques.

1.1.1. Major context: AI text generation

The primary scientific context for this work is the AI field of text generation. Text generation is a subfield of natural-language production although its boundaries are not easy to define exactly. Certainly the bottom end of text generation is the actual text itself, but at the top end the picture is not so clear. It will be assumed that natural-language production consists roughly of two stages that perhaps operate in parallel: text planning and text generation. The text planner is responsible for dividing up and ordering the conceptual input to the language production facility. The text generator takes the resulting chunks of semantic/pragmatic representation and transforms them into the desired natural language (English will be assumed throughout).

There are two major text-generation objectives that will be stressed here. The first is that the text generator should include an explicit grammar written in an established linguistic formalism. This allows the grammar to be written, understood, modified, judged and so on, independently of the rest of the text-generation system. It also facilitates linguistic contributions to the project from other sources.

A second objective of AI text generation is to develop systems that are practical. The current interest in expert systems, and the important claim that expert systems can explain their reasoning, means that proficient text-generation systems are urgently needed for practical application. The urgency is increasing as expert systems are adopted in socially oriented domains such as medicine and law. To be practical in this sense, the text generator must have good linguistic coverage, and it must be fast. Given that the linguistic coverage will be provided by a linguistic grammar (see previous point), the coverage is purely a linguistic problem and will not be addressed here. The speed of the generation is, however, extremely relevant. This constraint requires that the text generation be controlled by the most sophisticated computational techniques available. For this kind of problem, the most sophisticated and efficient computational techniques are those used in AI knowledge-based problem solving.

Unfortunately, there appears to be a conflict in the two objectives just mentioned. Established linguistic formalisms use highly specialized representations developed for linguistic purposes. AI problem solving also uses highly-specialized representations, but these were developed instead for computational purposes. The problem is that these two sets of highly specialized representations (not surprisingly) appear to be incompatible. A crucial objective of AI text-generation research is thus to interface the linguistic and problem-solving representations so that the other two objectives can both be met.

1.1.2. Minor context: functional linguistics

The nature of the text-generation task—finding grammatical constructs that satisfy semantic/pragmatic goals—suggests that a functional linguistic approach is most appropriate. A functional approach to linguistics views language in terms of what the speaker can do with it; it attempts to tie language to the social purposes for which it is used. The linguistic theory used throughout this work— systemic grammar—is a functional theory. It is therefore important that the grammars described here, and indeed the linguistic theory itself, not be judged by structural or generative criteria. The functional framework also means that there are several terms used here in an unorthodox manner. Systemic grammar, the concepts and terms, are discussed in Chapter 3.

1.2. Important assumptions

Having defined the context of this work, and explicitly stated that the linguistic coverage is a problem that will not be addressed, it must be pointed out that a vital assumption has been made here. Although the grammar implemented for this project is relatively large, it still has very limited coverage. An assumption has been made that systemic grammar, with enough work and development, can adequately describe the grammar of natural language for the purposes of text generation. A more precarious assumption has also been made, viz. that the semantic component of systemic theory is adequate. The justification for these assumptions is discussed in §8.2.

1.3. Specific overview

At this point a brief outline of the remaining chapters should be given. The book is roughly divided into three sections. The first three chapters (including this one) provide the background and introduce the relevant terms and concepts. The next two chapters form the core of the book—they put forward the new approach to text generation, first as an intuitive argument, then as a formal model. The final three chapters support and consolidate these ideas by illustration, comparison and discussion.

The title of Chapter 2 is "Background I: AI problem solving." This should not be interpreted as background to the field in general, but rather as background to those problem-solving terms and concepts that play a major role in the following discussion. The primary purpose of this chapter is to introduce the key concepts of *search* and *compilation*.

Chapter 3 is also a background chapter; it provides the background to systemic grammar. Again the treatment is heavily biased toward the terms and concepts that are important later on. This chapter also provides a brief history of the development of systemic theory to vindicate some of the less orthodox ideas. Examples are provided to illustrate the key concepts.

Chapter 4 is the crux of the work. Here the special relationship between AI problem solving and systemic grammar is unfolded and developed into an approach to text generation that surmounts the problem of interfacing AI problem-solving methods and an established linguistic formalism. This "Systemic Linguistic Approach to Natural-language Generation" (SLANG) is then illustrated by working through an example in some detail.

One disadvantage of systemic grammar is that it has never been formalized as more traditional grammars have. This makes it difficult to provide a formal model for this approach to text generation. These problems are remedied in Chapter 5: "The formal model." Formal definitions of a systemic grammar, a systemic syntactic structure, and the language generated by a systemic grammar are provided, and a formal treatment of the new generation method is given. Proofs relating to the soundness and completeness of the generation method are among the results derived from the model.

The text-generation, problem-solving and linguistic ideas appearing in this work have been implemented in a test system: SLANG-I. This implementation is described in detail in Chapter 6. The description is supplemented by a discussion of the limitations of the implementation and some thoughts on alternative implementations.

Chapter 7 compares SLANG with other recent approaches to text generation. A scheme for classifying text-generation systems is presented, and SLANG is shown to combine successfully the positive attributes of both the major text-generation classes.

Finally, Chapter 8 provides a summary of the book and some thoughts toward the future. Both the problems that may obstruct future work, and some potential extensions and offshoots, are examined.

Three appendices have been included at the end of the book. Appendix A, a supplement to Chapter 6, is a brief tutorial on OPS5—the implementation language of SLANG-I. Appendix B is a collection of sample texts produced by SLANG-I. Appendix C contains excerpts from the grammar used in SLANG-I.

2
Background I: AI problem solving

This chapter is intended to provide the background required to understand the AI aspects of the text-generation method presented in Chapter 4. This introduction will not be a comprehensive survey, but rather a primer to specific concepts and perspectives relevant to the generation method. First, the architecture of AI problem solving will be outlined. Second, the *search-space* model will be introduced and some search methods will be examined. Third, the idea of *knowledge compilation* will be explored, emphasizing the key role played by compiled knowledge in AI problem solving.

2.1. The architecture of AI problem solving

This discussion of the architecture of AI problem solving will have several limitations and biases—it will address AI problem solving as it is manifested in practical AI projects (especially expert systems), and it will be strongly biased toward the architecture and representations adopted in Chapter 6.

While the architecture of AI problem solving corresponds to some degree to the computer-science architecture—a program processing data—(see Brownston et al., 1985, p. 56), this correspondence is more likely to be misleading than helpful here. The architecture of AI problem solving involves three major components—the knowledge base, the inference engine, and the data memory or working memory. It must be assumed that any given problem solver will have been constructed to operate in some specific problem area or *domain*. Information about the classification of domain objects, the properties associated with these classes, the operations that can be performed within the domain, and other invariant domain-specific knowledge is stored in the knowledge base. The general rules of inference to be used in the problem solving (e.g. deduction) will be embodied in the inference engine. Although certain inference techniques may be included or omitted because of the nature of the problems being solved, the inference techniques will typically not be specific to any particular domain. A relatively small group of inference techniques are used to cover a wide range of AI problem-solving applications (for a survey, see Stefik et al., 1983a, 1983b). Information concerning the specific problem instance at hand—including intermediate results—is stored in working memory. Although there are, for instance, techniques for allowing efficient access to working memory, the details of working memory have little to do with the actual problem solving, and will not be discussed here.

Problem solving, then, consists of the inference engine using the knowledge in the knowledge base, together with the information in working memory, to make inferences that may lead to a solution to a given problem. As a simple illustration, suppose the fact that a certain entity X is a whale is recorded in working memory. The knowledge base may contain the knowledge that all whales are mammals and that all mammals are warm-blooded. Using this knowledge, the inference engine can infer that X is a mammal and hence warm-blooded.

The knowledge in the knowledge base can be represented in many ways. The representation which will be discussed here is the *production system*. A production system represents knowledge as a collection of rules, each consisting of two parts—the antecedent and consequent, also called the conditions and effects, also called the left-hand side and the right-hand side. The notation used for production rules is usually either "If *antecedent* then *consequent*", or "*antecedent —> consequent*", e.g. "If X is a mammal then X is warm-blooded."

Unlike a typical computer program, productions in the knowledge base are not a sequence of instructions to be processed one after another. The knowledge base should be viewed as a collection of productions, the order of which is completely irrelevant. As the problem solving proceeds, the inference engine simply picks appropriate productions from wherever they are in the knowledge base. How the inference engine decides which productions are appropriate will be discussed in the next section.

The advantage of the production system model is the ability to encode large amounts of knowledge as small, relatively independent packages. Each package is, by itself, easily understood, and easily included in, or deleted from, the knowledge base. When the problem domain requires that a wide variety of states and factors be considered, the production model is especially useful (Brownston et al., 1985, p. 25). Also, as Brownston et al. observe (ibid., p. 20), "[O]ne of the most important features of production systems [is that] they represent knowledge explicitly in chunks (that is, rules) that seem to be just the right size for capturing the steps that people employ when attacking non-trivial problems." This is particularly important in the construction of expert systems since bits of knowledge used by human experts can easily be encoded as production rules. Examples of production rules will be given in §2.2.3 below.

2.2. The search-space model

The previous section introduced the architecture of AI problem solving, and described how the inference engine makes inferences from working memory using the knowledge in the knowledge base. Now it is certainly not intended that the inference engine be provided with knowledge of a domain and asked to make all possible inferences—the number of results would simply be too large. It is more practical, in AI problem solving, for the problem solver to be given a specific problem, and to do as little inference as possible to find a solution. Many types of AI problem solving can best be understood as a *search* in a problem space or search space. The search-space problem-solving model will now be discussed in terms of the production-rule representation introduced above.

The problem space, or search space, is like a maze. During the search for a solution to a particular problem, there are alternative paths the problem solver can take (alternative inferences to be made from the knowledge and data). Some of these paths lead directly toward a solution, but many more lead to dead ends (e.g. the inferring of conflicting results), or to a solution via an unnecessarily long route (e.g. the inferring of irrelevant results). The objective of AI problem-solving research has been to develop search methods that lead to a solution as quickly as possible, avoiding dead ends and unnecessarily long routes, while minimizing the amount of decision time required at the many crossroads. A few of these methods will now be surveyed.

2.2.1. *Brute-force search*

One search method often used for computer-science applications is the *depth-first* search. This is a method by which Theseus could have exploited Ariadne's thread to search the maze of the Minotaur. At each point in the search where a choice is required, each alternative is recursively explored in order (say from left to right). So Theseus begins, and at each choice point he takes the leftmost path and continues, unwinding Ariadne's thread as he goes. When he encounters a dead end, he simply follows the thread back—*backtracks*—to the most recent choice point, marks the bad path, and takes the next path to the right. If all the alternatives are marked as bad, he follows the thread back to the still previous choice point and marks the path as bad, takes the next path to the right, and so on.

Depth-first search is one of a class of search techniques called *brute-force* or *blind* search because they are simply methods for systematically eliminating every possibility (for a more detailed discussion of some of these techniques, see Barr et al., 1981, pp. 38-40). These methods may be adequate for problems where the number of alternatives is small, but they are inadequate for any interesting AI applications because they are not selective enough—it takes too long to explore so many paths.

2.2.2. *Heuristic search*

Often, during search, all the alternatives are not equally promising, given a particular set of solution criteria. An "evaluation function" can sometimes be found that can indicate preference for particular alternatives as the search proceeds. The search can then immediately focus on the most promising of the alternatives, ignoring the others—at least as long as the promise is sustained. The advantage of such *heuristic* search over brute-force search is that by not exploring unlikely paths, the solution is often found much sooner.

There are, however, some problems with this type of heuristic search. For many domains it is difficult to find a suitable evaluation function. Also, if the function is expensive to compute—in particular if it must take into consideration many complex interactions—the benefits of heuristic search are lost.

Suppose (following Bundy, 1983, p. 54), Theseus needs to be at a certain position to satisfy the solution criteria. An evaluation function could be devised that would favour moves toward this position. Now suppose Theseus is to collect an object and return to the original position. In this case the evaluation function would not work because he must move away from the desired position in order to collect the object. The function could perhaps be modified to take into account the distance between Theseus and the object, but suppose more than one object is to be collected. Even if a function could be written that takes everything into account, it would be so expensive to compute that it would be doing all the work instead of the heuristic search mechanism. Applying large amounts of knowledge to work out interactions is not a bad idea, but in this case the problem-solving process is no longer this kind of simple heuristic search.

2.2.3. Forward-chaining

One way to ensure that Theseus quickly finds his way to any given point in the maze would be to provide him with very specific knowledge about the choice points—perhaps actually telling him which choice to make in many cases. If the knowledge is to be represented in terms of production rules, this would mean having many rules, each with very specific antecedents, or conditions of applicability. At each choice point only a small number of antecedents will be satisfied (perhaps only one), so the problem solver has only a small number of rules from which the next inference can be made. This kind of specific knowledge reduces the number of guesses the problem solver must make and thereby reduces the time required for the search.

One method of reasoning with this kind of detailed knowledge is *forward-chaining*. During the problem-solving process, the inference engine looks for a rule whose antecedent or condition is currently satisfied. Often this condition will involve very specific problem characteristics to be present, or may even require that a certain phase of the problem-solving process is underway. The consequent, or effects, of the rule may make subtle changes to working memory that result in specific rules becoming applicable that were not applicable before, or result in spoiling some rules' applicability. At each step a rule is chosen whose conditions are satisfied, its effects are executed, another rule whose conditions are satisfied by the new situation is chosen as the next link in the chain of inferences and so on. This is called forward-chaining because the problem solver begins at the start of the maze and works forward toward a solution.

As an example of a rule that could be used for forward-chaining, consider the following rule from a medical-diagnosis expert system (from Stefik et al., 1983b, p. 93). Note that the sample rules in this chapter are expressed as English paraphrases to avoid unnecessary notation.

<pre>
If   the infection is primary-bacteremia, and
        the site of the culture is one of the sterile sites, and
        the suspected portal of entry of the organism is the
        gastro-intestinal tract,
then   there is suggestive evidence (0.7) that the identity of the
        organism is bacteroids.
</pre>

The inference engine could forward-chain from an initial set of data towards a diagnosis, and the above rule may appear in the middle of the chain of reasoning. Other rules (appearing earlier in the chain) would have had effects placing each of the three conditions in working memory (e.g. "... then the suspected portal of entry of the organism is the gastro-intestinal tract"). Still other rules (appearing later in the chain) may have conditions of the form: "If there is suggestive evidence that the identity of the organism is bacteroids, and ..."

Another forward-chaining rule from a medical expert system (the Ventilator Manager, from ibid., p. 98) is

<pre>
If   the current context "Assist," and
        the respiration rate has been stable for 20 minutes, and
        the I/EW ratio has been stable for 20 minutes,
then   the patient is on CMV [controlled mandatory ventilation].
</pre>

Still another example is from R1—an expert system for configuring computers (from ibid., p. 103):

> If   the most current active context is assigning a power supply, and
> a UNIBUS adaptor has been put in a cabinet, and
> the position it occupies in the cabinet (its nexus) is known, and
> there is space available in the cabinet for a power supply for that
> nexus, and
> there is an available power supply, and
> there is no H7101 regulator available,
> then add an H7101 regulator to the order.

Note that in each of these cases the conditions are very specific. This gives the forward-chaining inference engine little or no room for making inappropriate inferences (taking bad paths in the maze).

2.2.4. Goal-directed backward-chaining

An often useful technique for solving mazes (or similar problems) is to start at the solution and work backward. This is also a useful technique for AI problem solving with production rules. Given a certain problem to solve—a goal—the inference engine looks for a rule whose effects directly achieve the goal. Now remember that production rules have two parts, and this production rule will probably have conditions that are not satisfied. These conditions are simply set as subgoals, and the problem solver will attempt to solve them in the same way. The problem solver thus reduces the original problem to a set of (hopefully simpler) subproblems—this is called *problem reduction* (see Nilsson, 1971, pp. 80-123). If the problem solver is successful, the problem will eventually reduce to a set of problems whose solutions are already known, or which can be solved directly using a rule whose effects satisfy the subgoal and whose conditions are already satisfied. Using production rules to form a chain of inferences from a goal back to the start is called goal-directed *backward-chaining* (Brownston et al., 1985, Glossary).

The following is an example of a backward-chaining rule for the monkey and bananas problem (adapted from Brownston et al., 1985, p. 390):

> If   the ladder is on the floor under the object
> and the monkey is on the ladder
> and the monkey is holding nothing
> and there is no object on the goal object
> then modify the monkey to indicate it is holding the object.

If there is a goal for the monkey to be holding some bananas which are on the ceiling, the inference engine could use the above rule to achieve the goal, but it will also have to set the four conditions as subgoals and solve them. The resulting chain of inferences will form a plan for the monkey to get the bananas.

Another example is from an expert system for chemical spills (from Waterman and Hayes-Roth, 1983, p. 175-6):

> If   1) the location where the spill was first reported
>   is not the source,
>   2) the liquid is flowing, and
>   3) the spill basin is known,
> then determine suggestions for discovering the source
>   of the spill by backtracking from the spill basin,
>   or, failing that, determine the node farthest back
>   in the drainage network to which the spill has
>   been traced.

In this case the goal is "determine suggestions for discovering the source of the spill." An attempt is made to satisfy the conditions in the left-hand side of the rule, and if successful, the right-hand side will be executed.

Note that there is no difference in the form of the rules used for forward- and backward-chaining. The direction the chaining should take for problem solving will depend on the nature of the conditions and effects of the rules. Suppose a collection of rules all contain disjunctive effects, e.g. If you are at point A then go to either point B or to point C (or equivalently, two rules: If you are at point A then go to point B; If you are at point A then go to point C). Forward-chaining will not help here because the problem solver has no basis for choosing between the disjuncts. But note that backward-chaining will work because regardless of whether the goal is to get to point B or to point C, the next step backward is to point A. Suppose another set of rules contains disjunctive conditions, e.g. If you are at point A or point B then go to point C. In this case backward-chaining will not work well because given the goal point C, the problem solver has no way of choosing which of A or B should be set as the subgoal. Forward-chaining works well in this case since regardless of whether the current location is point A or point B, the next step should be point C.

These, of course, have only been the extreme cases. Many knowledge bases are such that both forward- and backward-chaining should be used to solve the problem. Forward-chaining rules may explicitly set goals as some of their effects, and backward-chaining rules may have side effects (effects other than the one matching the goal) that help satisfy the conditions of some of the forward-chaining rules. The inference engine can simply make both forward and backward inferences as the opportunities arise.

This section has introduced the central concept of *search*. Some search techniques were surveyed, contrasting the inexpedient brute-force techniques with forward- and backward-chaining which, when given the necessary knowledge, quickly guide the problem solver to a solution.

2.3. Knowledge compilation

Compiled knowledge. Knowledge that encodes rules of inference in which implied chains of reasoning are suppressed for the sake of efficiency. (Brownston et al., 1985, Glossary)

The discussion, thus far, has provided a brief and basic introduction to the central concepts of AI problem solving. At this point, there is one important concept—*knowledge compilation*—that needs some special attention. This attention is warranted by the extensive use of compiled knowledge in expert systems, and by the key role compiled knowledge plays in the text-generation method described in Chapter 4.

2.3.1. Compilation and granularity

The concept of compilation, as it is used in the context of problem-solving knowledge, can perhaps best be explained in terms of the notion of *granularity* (e.g. Hobbs, 1985). Granularity, or grain size, is a property that applies to both objects and operations. Consider a brick wall—there are several different grain sizes at which the wall can be represented. It could be represented as one giant grain, or as a collection of bricks, or as a large collection of clay particles. The operation of constructing a brick wall can also be represented as a piece-by-piece process at any of these grain sizes. Several operations at one granularity can be *compiled* to form one operation at a larger grain size. Many operations involving clay particles are compiled to form the large-grain operation of laying a brick. The laying of a brick achieves, in one operation, what would take many operations at a finer granularity. No work magically disappears—the point is simply that it is easier to build a wall if given bricks than if given clay, because the brick manufacturer has already done most of the work. As a result of the compilation performed at the brick factory, the builder is able to work with larger grains and therefore achieve more with each step.

The same principles apply to AI problem solving, which was earlier characterized as the construction of a chain of inferences between two points. It is much easier to construct a chain between two points, if a few large links are used rather than many small ones. A medical student may be able to infer a certain diagnosis through a long and complex reasoning process using general principles. A medical expert may be able to reach the same conclusion much more quickly using compiled knowledge explicitly associating specific combinations of symptoms with specific diseases. Each of the large-grained inferences made by the expert corresponds to many fine-grained inferences made by the novice, who follows detailed causal chains between diseases and symptoms. But note that the expert does not actually make the fine-grained inferences any more than the bricklayer makes the bricks he uses. The expert is quicker than the novice because his knowledge allows fewer inferences to be made, as a result of reasoning at a larger grain size.

> [T]he quality true experts seem to possess that laymen do not is an ability to recognize large-scale patterns and jump quickly to reasonable hypotheses. Expert behavior seems to demand that blind search through large numbers of hypotheses be avoided in favor of quick elimination of many possibilities in each inferential move.
>
> High-level macromoves that allow large amounts of ground to be covered in each step are a key feature of all the expert systems that have been built to date. (Brachman et al., 1983, pp. 44)

Usually a compiled inference provides a complete solution to a particular part of the problem—it represents a large link in the metaphorical chain of inferences. A related technique involves rules that only represent the blueprint of a large link, not the link itself. Although such rules do not have as much knowledge compiled into them, they still represent useful compiled knowledge because the blueprints will indicate which links will fit together—avoiding the construction of links that will not fit into the solution chain. Once the problem has been solved at the coarse granularity using the blueprints, the subproblems become the construction of the individual links in the chain. The problem solving then proceeds to successively finer granularities. This idea is the basis of hierarchical planning (e.g. Sacerdoti, 1975; Tate, 1976).

In any case, the use of compiled knowledge greatly enhances the problem solver's ability to solve the problem quickly, because more is accomplished with each inference.

2.3.2. Sources of compiled knowledge

The importance of compiled knowledge has been established, but the question of how that knowledge is acquired has not been addressed. The three major sources of compiled knowledge will be mentioned here.

The first, and most common, source of compiled knowledge is a human expert. During the construction of an expert system, human experts are interviewed extensively to discover, *inter alia,* the large-grain-size rules they employ when solving problems. These rules can seldom be consciously accessed by the human expert—they usually must be extracted by having the expert think aloud, and asking the expert detailed questions about specific cases (see Buchanan et al., 1983, p. 164).

A second source of compiled knowledge is the builder of the expert system. If certain subproblems are repeatedly occurring, and the solutions to these subproblems are expensive to compute, then the solutions may be hand-coded as large-grain-size rules that will allow each of the subproblems to be solved in a single step.

A third source of compiled knowledge is automatic compilation. Rules with a large grain size tend to be awkward, difficult to understand, difficult to modify and so on. These problems can be avoided by working with knowledge at one granularity, then automatically compiling the knowledge into larger grains. Probably the best known example of automatic knowledge compilation is the MACROP (macro operator) facility in the STRIPS problem solver (see Bundy, 1983, pp. 60-2; Barr et al., 1981, pp. 131-4). The basic idea is that after constructing a plan to achieve some task, the plan is generalized (by replacing specific tokens with variables where possible) and saved for future use. The next time the problem arises it can be solved directly using the MACROP. The more of these MACROPS that have been saved, the less work the planner has to do on the fine details—the grain size of the planner's work increases.

Another type of automatic knowledge compilation is to have a preprocessor that takes a rule-base and compiles it into larger, more efficient rules before any problem solving is done. This technique, like the construction of MACROPS, has the advantage that the knowledge engineer does not have to write, modify, understand etc., rules with too coarse a granularity (see Brownston et al., 1985, pp. 263-4).

> The promise of knowledge compilation ideas is to make it possible to use very general means for representing knowledge while an expert system is being build and debugged. Then a compiler can be applied to make this knowledge base efficient enough to compete with hand-coding. (Stefik et al., 1983b, p. 120)

2.3.3. Reasoning from first principles

After the initial success of expert systems that relied on compiled knowledge, there has recently been an interest in "reasoning from first principles." This type of reasoning is used to supplement the reasoning with compiled knowledge, primarily for reasons of robustness and explanation.

> The principle quality that general knowledge and inferential ability produces, over and above what expert rules do is *robustness*. As new, unanticipated patterns crop up, inflexible, compiled solutions fail. General problem-solving abilities allow a more graceful degradation at the outer edges of domain knowledge—a kind of conceptual extrapolation—as well as permit interpolation between high-level rules that are not complete within the domain....
>
> It should be noted that this type of knowledge is essentially the antithesis of high-level macro-move expertise. It is knowledge that is explicitly *not* compiled, so that it may support general inferential procedures. Applying knowledge with general methods, however, is inevitably slower than using multi-step inferential rules. (Hayes-Roth et al., 1983, p. 46)

Returning to the bricks and clay analogy, there are many types of structures for which bricks are not suitable (e.g. pottery, statues). The fine-grained clay, however is much more flexible. But again, using clay is inevitably slower than using bricks in cases where bricks are suitable.

This "reasoning from first principles" has also been advocated for providing explanations of high-level reasoning.

> Explanation in expert systems is usually associated with some form of tracing of rules that fire during the course of a problem-solving session. This is about the closest to real explanation that today's systems can come, given the fact that their knowledge is represented almost exclusively as high-level rules. However, a satisfactory explanation of how a conclusion was derived demands an ability to connect the inference steps with fundamental domain principles as justifications.... Each high-level macromove can be justified only by recourse to the basic principles that make it sound—the rule cannot be its own justification. (Brachman et al., 1983, p. 48)

It must be stressed, however, that AI problem solving will always rely on compiled knowledge whenever possible for reasons of efficiency. Only when no applicable compiled knowledge is available, or when detailed explanations are required, will reasoning from first principles be called for.

2.4. Summary

This chapter has introduced the AI problem-solving concepts that will be needed in later chapters. The general architecture of AI problem solving was presented, followed by a discussion of production rules as a representation of problem-solving knowledge. The concept of a search-space was outlined using the analogy of searching a maze. Several search methods were surveyed, with emphasis on forward- and backward-chaining of production rules. Finally, issues surrounding the compilation and granularity of problem-solving knowledge were examined.

AI problem solving is a rapidly developing and already complex field, and this chapter could offer only a narrow perspective on a few of the important ideas. Nevertheless, this brief introduction will hopefully have shed enough light to make clear the significance of the problem-solving issues raised in later chapters.

3
Background II: systemic grammar

Any work on text generation must give an account of the linguistic theory—adopted or created—on which the generation process operates. This chapter is an introduction to the linguistic theory adopted here—systemic grammar. The linguistic representation plays a particularly important role in this work. Indeed, an understanding of many of the computational text-generation ideas requires an understanding of the underlying concepts in systemic theory.

This introduction to systemic grammar begins with a short history focused on the major contributors: Malinowski, Firth, Hjelmslev and Halliday. Then the goals or aims of systemic grammar are outlined. Some of the concepts from systemic theory which are most relevant to this work are then discussed in detail. Finally, descriptions of the stratification of systemic grammar, and in particular of the semantic stratum, are given.

3.1. History

3.1.1. Malinowski (1884-1942)

The origins of systemic linguistics clearly lie in the work of the anthropologist and ethnographer Bronislaw Malinowski (e.g. 1923). From Malinowski come two ideas that have had a profound influence on systemic theory. The first is the observation of the inseparability of language and its social and cultural context (Whorf must also be credited as an influence on this point—Kress, 1976, pp. ix-x). Malinowski argued that language could only be viewed and explained with reference to the social and cultural milieu. It is important to note the sharp contrast between this starting point of systemic linguistics and the starting point of the structural/formal tradition: that language is a self-contained system (ibid., p. viii). Most importantly here, Malinowski provided the idea of "context of situation"—a description of the contextual factors influencing an utterance.

The second important idea from Malinowski is that language is "functional"—it is used to perform certain functions in society. Of particular note is his grouping of the functions of a particular language into broad categories. One such category found in the Polynesian societies studied by Malinowski is the "magical function" where language is used to control the environment (ibid., p. viii).

Malinowski's influence remained unmistakable as his ideas were refined and developed by others. The first step in the refinement process was to transfer the thinking of the anthropologist into a linguistic framework.

3.1.2. Firth (1890-1960)

It was the linguist J. R. Firth who took Malinowski's ideas and adapted them so they could fit into a linguistic theory. In particular he accepted the close relationship between language and society put forward by the anthropologist.

> Malinowski's notions were further developed and made explicit by Firth ... who maintained that the context of situation was not to be interpreted in concrete terms as a sort of audiovisual record of the surrounding 'props' but was, rather, an abstract representation of the environment in terms of certain general categories having relevance to the text. (Halliday, 1978, p. 109)

One key notion in Firth's work was the concept of "system" (from which systemic grammar eventually took its name)—a set of linguistic choices in a specific linguistic context (ibid., p. xiii). Firth's emphasis on differentiating (according to de Saussure's dichotomy) this "paradigmatic" (system-based) description and the "syntagmatic" (structure-based) description set him apart from the Bloomfieldian tradition (Halliday and Martin, 1981, p. 19).

Firth realized that words or sentences could not just be related directly to a general context, but rather the context had to be divided up into different levels—as he said, like "breaking white light into a spectrum" (Monaghan, 1979, p. 185). Thus the phonological choices must be made in a phonological context, grammatical choices must be made in a grammatical context and so on.

Another key observation was that the general situation types described by Malinowski resulted in a "multiplicity of languages" within a language as a whole (Kress, 1976, p. xiv). This insight later led Halliday to the important concept of *register* (see §3.5).

3.1.3. Hjelmslev (1899-1965)
Louis Hjelmslev was a contemporary of Firth's, but although their work shared some important characteristics (e.g. an emphasis on paradigmatic description), their influence on systemic grammar was independent. Hjelmslev's contribution comes from his work on the *realizational* view of language (e.g. Hjelmslev, 1961—original Danish version 1943). Halliday says there are two ways of thinking about language, "There is the *realizational* view, language as one system coded in another and recoded in another; and the *combinational* view, where language is seen as larger units made up of smaller units" (Halliday, 1978, p. 42).

Semantics, grammar, and phonology, are all, according to Hjelmslev, *semiotics* or sign systems. Signs at one level can be recoded—or realized by—signs at a lower level. The significance of the realizational approach, from this historical perspective, is that it allows the organizations at the various levels to be completely independent of one another. The compositional representation of a sequence of phrases necessarily reflects the clausal organization. In contrast, the realizational representation at the phoneme level (in particular if represented paradigmatically in terms of phonological choices) need not reflect the representation at the grammatical level at all. Perhaps more significantly, the semantic and grammatical representations need not reflect each other—e.g. the semantics can be organized by socio-semantic criteria, and the grammar can be organized by functional grammatical criteria.

Hjelmslev's insights into the theory of language had a considerable influence on the development of systemic linguistics, and his realizational approach became a cornerstone of systemic grammar.

3.1.4. Halliday (1925-)
A student of Firth's, M. A. K. Halliday, took the concept of *system* and refined it so the context of the choice is paradigmatic (related to other choices) rather than a place in structure. Also, "Firth did not provide a set of terms or categories which could systematically relate all the descriptive statements on all levels to each other" (Kress, 1976, p. xv), so Halliday felt Firth's work needed to be "underpinned" by a more rigorous model. "Lamb's stratification theory [see

Winograd, 1983, pp. 299-301], with its Hjelmslevian basis, provides this, and gives a systematic account of linguistic levels ..." (Halliday, 1976a, p. 26). Halliday brought all this together to form a linguistic theory (originally presented in 1961) that eventually became known as "systemic grammar." Later work included a linguistic formalism—system networks—and the work on register stemming from Firth's "multiplicity of languages."

Halliday's approach specifically pushes structure into the background using the paradigmatic and realizational descriptions pioneered by Firth and Hjelmslev, as a means of stressing the functional perspective on language initiated by Malinowski. The remainder of this chapter will relate, in some detail, Halliday's theory of systemic grammar.

3.2. The goals of systemic grammar

The previous sections have shown that the origins of systemic grammar differ significantly from those of the currently dominant school of linguistics. The roots of systemic grammar

> ... were in anthropology and sociology, not in mathematics or formal logic. The questions that motivated its development were not those of grammaticality or the acquisition of linguistic competence, but those of language as a social activity: *What are the social functions of language? How does language fulfill these social functions? How does language work?* (Winograd, 1983, p. 273)

Some of the relevant goals of systemic grammar result from the historical interests introduced in the previous sections. The first of these is the goal of describing the functions of language. There are several levels at which this description must be made. On one hand there is what might be called the semantic function—an utterance functions as a question or a statement, or part of an utterance may identify the performer of an action or what is being talked about. On the other hand there is what might be called the syntactic function—the "subject" of a clause, the "head" of a nominal-group and so on. Thus one goal of systemic grammar is to capture the subtle relationship between the semantic function, the syntactic function and the form itself (ibid., p. 277).

> The functional description of a mechanism says what it *does*. The implementation description says *how it does it*. The implementation description of the frame of which it is a part says *what it is used for*. If you want to understand in more detail, then the interface information, represented either explicitly or inherited from the implementation model, tells you how the functions of the parts come together to implement the

total behaviour. If you want to understand in still more detail, you recurse and examine the functions of the subparts in the same way. Etc. ad infinitum. (Smith, 1978, p. 31)

[W]e are taking a functional view of language, in the sense that we are interested in what language can do, or rather in what the speaker, child or adult, can do with it; and that we try to explain the nature of language, its internal organization and patterning, in terms of the functions that it has evolved to serve. (Halliday in deJoia and Stenton, 1080, §193)

Another goal of systemic grammar that has important consequences in later chapters is the *classification* of both social meaning and linguistic forms. This classification "plays a major theoretical role in systemic grammar" (Winograd, 1983, p. 276). It was suggested above that even classification, which is manifested by paradigmatic description, serves linguistically to facilitate functional description by abstracting away from structure. Thus functional description is clearly the driving force behind systemic theory.

Now the emphasis on functional description in systemic grammar leaves the theory open to criticism from mainstream linguistics with *its* emphasis on description of structure. But it should be understood that the two approaches to linguistic study are complementary, not conflicting. A good analogy can be drawn, in this regard, between linguistic description and biological description.

Functional description is a basic cognitive tool. Consider the problem of writing a 'grammar for animals'—a formalism that describes what their pieces are and how they fit together. In doing this, biologists look for functional systems, such as the skeletal system, the muscular system and the circulatory system. Individual structures are then described in the context of these different systems and the roles they play in them. Indeed, anatomy could be studied without any reference to this 'physiological' level of description. An animal can be seen as a complex interweaving of cords, tubes, bones, fibers etc. But to do so would make the structure seem impossibly complex and arbitrary. The key to understanding the complexity of the structure lies in recognizing its functional organization. The old adage that 'form follows function' can serve as a framework for understanding language. (Winograd, 1983, p. 279)

In biology, the functional approach taken by physiology and the structural approach taken by regional anatomy are complementary. Systemic grammar is not, and should not be viewed as, a theory of the structure of language. It is a functional theory, and in this capacity makes a valuable contribution to the study of language.

3.3. Important concepts in systemic grammar

A brief look at the history and goals of systemic grammar has been presented, and an introduction to the theory itself will now be given. This will not be a thorough linguistic treatment, but will attempt to provide some insight into the concepts from systemic grammar that play a significant role in the remainder of this work. A good general overview of systemic grammar can be found in (Winograd, 1983, Chapter 6).

3.3.1. Feature

Probably the best starting point is the notion of a "feature." One of the primary goals of systemic grammar is classification (see §3.2 above) and a feature can be defined as the name of a class (Halliday and Martin, 1981, Glossary). Some features of the clause (classes to which a clause may belong), are *declarative, finite, benefactive, negative, interrogative, positive* and so on.

Now it should be apparent that these features are not all independent. If a clause has the feature *declarative* then it cannot also have the feature *interrogative*. Similarly if a clause is *negative* then it cannot also be *positive*. This leads to the concept of "system."

3.3.2. System

A system is a mutually exclusive set of classes (or features) and thus represents a choice or "potential." This description of language in terms of choices is the "paradigmatic" description mentioned above. Note that this is important from the point of view of classification and information theory—if a clause is labelled as *declarative* it also means that the clause is not *interrogative*.

The next step is to observe that a particular choice is not always applicable—e.g. a linguistic item is not always either *declarative* or *interrogative*. Thus some sort of context must be introduced to determine which choices are relevant when. For Firth, the context was a structural one—the relevant choices were directly dependent on the structure of the linguistic item. Halliday, however, made the radical step of defining the context in terms of other choices. For instance the choice between *declarative* and *interrogative* is only appropriate if the clause is *indicative* as opposed to *imperative*.

Often a choice will depend on a logical combination of features instead of on just one. In any case, the features that must be present for a system to be appropriate are called the "entry conditions" of the system. The system and entry condition relationships can be illustrated by drawing a "system network."

3.3.3. System network

System networks display graphically the relationships between features in the grammar. A system is illustrated by a "T" intersection (representing a choice between two or more features):

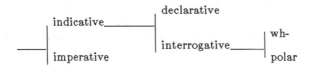

Entry conditions are illustrated by simply drawing lines from the entry conditions to the system:

Several features may be involved in entry condition relations. If either a feature acts as an entry condition to several systems or a particular system has several conjunctive entry conditions, this is illustrated with curly brackets, "{" and "}" respectively. Disjunctive (not necessarily exclusive) entry conditions are represented by a ("T" merge) "]-".

Consider Figure 3.1. Here there is a variety of complex relationships between features. Features are in lower case; system labels are in upper case and are merely for documentation. The feature *question* is the sole entry condition for the system containing *animate* and is a disjunctive entry condition for the CASE system. The feature *personal* is the entry condition for the PERSON system and a disjunctive entry condition for the CASE and NUMBER systems. The features *third* and *singular* must both be chosen if the system GENDER is to be relevant.

In addition to features which are terms in systems, there are features—called "gates"—which are simply dependent on some combination of other features, without choice. These could be thought of as degenerate systems with only one feature. The entry conditions of gates are represented in exactly the same way as those of systems.

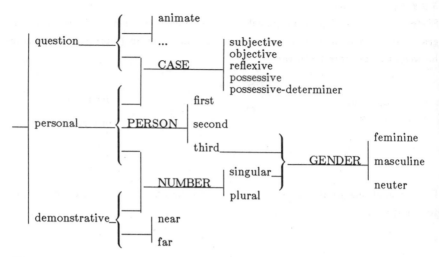

Figure 3.1. English pronouns (from Winograd, 1983, p. 293).

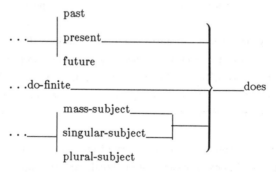

Figure 3.2. A gate from a clause network (Mann/Halliday).

In Figure 3.2, if the features *present* and *do-finite* have been chosen, and either *mass-subject* or *singular-subject* have been chosen, then the feature *does* is chosen as well—there is no choice here. The entry conditions to gates may be terms in systems or other gates: in Figure 3.2 *present, mass-subject,* and *singular-subject* are terms in systems, while *do-finite* is another gate.

Excerpts from the clause system network, and the pronoun system network (actually part of a larger noun network) have been presented. System networks are required for constituents such as the prepositional phrase, the clause-complex (roughly corresponding to a sentence) and so on. "The grammar itself thus takes the form of a series of system networks, where each network represents the choices available to a given constituent type ..." (deJoia and Stenton, 1980,

26

§685). Although there are clearly structural relationships between the types of constituents, the system networks allow a complete paradigmatic description—in terms of feature choices—to be given for any particular constituent without referring to its substructure at all.

3.3.4. Delicacy

> As with any classification system, a system network for syntactic objects can go to varying levels of detail. In biology, an organism that is assigned a species feature is more precisely described than one assigned only to a family or genus. The more precise the classification, the more information is available about the object. In systemic grammar, this scale of precision is called *delicacy*.... (Winograd, 1983, p. 296)

Delicacy applies to features and systems, and is clearly illustrated in system networks. Generally speaking, system networks increase in delicacy from left to right. Some of the delicacy relations in Figure 3.1 are: the feature *masculine* is more delicate than the feature *personal*; the system GENDER is more delicate than the system NUMBER; the features *subjective* and *objective* are of equal delicacy; and the system whose terms are *question, personal* and *demonstrative* is the least delicate system.

3.3.5. Functional analysis

Another important concept in systemic linguistics is the idea of "function." Functional analysis in systemic grammar consists of more than just labelling linguistic items with terms like "Subject" and "Agent." The theory provides for analysis of several functional dimensions simultaneously, and indeed a large part of the linguistic description consists of relating these analyses.

	this gazebo	*was built*	*by*	*Sir Christopher Wren*
mood	Subject	Predicator		Adjunct
transitivity	Goal	Action		Actor
theme	Theme		Rheme	

Figure 3.3. Functional analyses of a clause (Winograd, 1983, p. 283).

Figure 3.3 shows three functional analyses of the same clause. Each function is associated with one type of analysis. The function Actor, for instance, is always used in the analysis of transitivity, and the function Subject is always used in the

27

analysis of mood. The different analyses are related by "conflating" functions from different analyses (e.g. Subject, Goal and Theme are all interpretations of *this gazebo* above).

A consequence of this multidimensional functional treatment is that there are in fact several constituent analyses associated with a linguistic item—one for each different functional analysis. This presentation will use four functional analyses: transitivity, ergativity, mood and theme.

The analysis of transitivity (see Halliday, 1985, pp. 101-44; Winograd, 1983, pp. 497-504) is an analysis of "process." The process *per se* is represented by the function Process (realized by "built" in Figure 3.3). The remainder of the set of functions depends on the nature of the process.

The first type of process is *material* (Halliday, 1985, pp. 102-6), a process of "doing" or "creating." The primary functions are Actor and Goal. A Beneficiary appears in the case of benefactive processes.

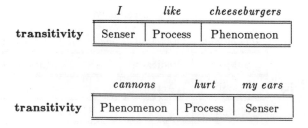

	Jack	*gave*	*the book*	*to*	*Janet*
transitivity	Actor	Process	Goal		Beneficiary

	the apples	*were*	*eaten*	*by*	*Jack*
transitivity	Goal		Process		Actor

If the process is *mental* (ibid., pp. 106-12) then the functions are the Process, the Senser, and the Phenomenon.

	I	*like*	*cheeseburgers*
transitivity	Senser	Process	Phenomenon

	cannons	*hurt*	*my ears*
transitivity	Phenomenon	Process	Senser

If the process is *verbal* (ibid., p. 129) then the functions are the Process, the Sayer and what is usually an embedded clause, Beta.

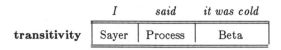

Finally, the process may be *relational* (ibid., pp. 112-28). There are two kinds of relational process, each with its own set of functions. There are *attributive* processes which involve an Attribute and a Carrier.

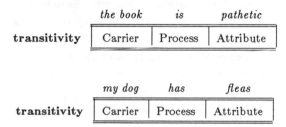

There are also the *identifying* processes which involve the functions Identifier and Identified.

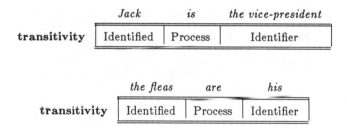

Halliday (1985, pp. 144-57) has argued that transitivity is no longer as important an analysis of English as it once was. The idea of transitivity is that there is a process and an Actor, and the question is whether or not the process extends beyond the Actor to something else (the Goal) (ibid., p. 145).

a) the gun fired (intransitive)

b) the gun fired the bullet (transitive)

Here "the gun" is the Actor in each case, and b) is transitive because the bullet is the Goal. However, according to Halliday the majority of high-frequency verbs that can be either transitive or intransitive, yield pairs such as:

a) the glass broke (intransitive)

b) the singer broke the glass (transitive)

Here the relationship isn't really transitivity at all. The process of the glass breaking in a) does not extend to the singer in b) as did the firing of the gun in the previous example. The distinction being made in this case is whether the process was "caused" or not—ergative or non-ergative processes respectively. The functions used for the ergative analysis are the Process, the Agent (called the Causer in some of the earlier literature), the Medium (earlier called the Affected), and perhaps the Beneficiary.

	the glass	*broke*
ergativity	Medium	Process
transitivity	Actor	Process

	the singer	*broke*	*the glass*
ergativity	Agent	Process	Medium
transitivity	Actor	Process	Goal

Notice that the Medium is constant in the above examples, whereas the Actor shifts in the transitivity analyses. Both the transitivity and ergativity analyses, as well as their interaction (sometimes the Medium is conflated with the Actor, sometimes with the Goal) are useful.

The functional analysis of mood (Halliday, 1985, pp. 68-100) is slightly more complex than that of either transitivity or ergativity. This is because there is more than one level of analysis. At the top level the functions used are: Mood, Residue and, optionally, Moodtag.

	the man has	*eaten the steak*
mood	Mood	Residue

	let's	*find the answer*	*shall we*
mood	Mood	Residue	Moodtag

Each of these functions is divided or "expanded" into a number of subfunctions. The Mood is expanded into the Subject and the Finite, the Residue is expanded into the Lexverb (this differs from much of the systemic literature) and the Residual, and the Moodtag is expanded into the Tagsubject and the Tagfinite.

	the man	*has*	*eaten*	*the steak*
mood	Subject	Finite	Lexverb	Residual
	Mood		Residue	

	let's	*find*	*the answer*	*shall*	*we*
mood	Subject	Lexverb	Residual	Tagfinite	Tagsubject
	Mood	Residue		Moodtag	

Like the analysis of mood, the analysis of theme (ibid., pp. 38-67) involves several layers of functions. At the top layer are the functions Theme and Rheme. The Rheme is not expanded further, but the Theme is expanded into the Textual, the Interpersonal, and the Topical. These are expanded further in Halliday (1985) but the further subdivisions are not used here. The Topical is usually conflated with the Subject, the Interpersonal is a modal adjunct (ibid., p. 50), and the Textual is a conjunction or conjunctive adjunct (ibid., and especially Halliday and Hasan, 1976, Chapter 5).

	perhaps	*my team*	*will win*
theme	Interpersonal	Topical	
	Theme		Rheme

	in other words	*to be honest*	*they*	*are bad*
theme	Textual	Interpersonal	Topical	
	Theme			Rheme

Another functional analysis is important when working with speech. This is the analysis of "information structure" and involves the functions Given and New (Halliday, 1985, pp. 274-51; Winograd, 1983, pp. 505-6). The portion of a "tone group" (often a clause) conveying information already possessed by the hearer functions as Given; the portion of the tone group conveying information new to the hearer functions as New. Information analysis is germane to issues of stress, intonation and word order. Since the information analysis is largely concerned with speech issues, it has been excluded from this work to avoid the added complexity.

The functional analysis of the group is much less complex than that of the clause. Although relatively complex group analyses are provided by Halliday (1985, pp. 159-75), the simpler analyses given in Halliday (1976b, pp. 131-5) are used here. The only substantial group network used is the nominal-group, because the verbal-group is treated in the analysis of the clause. The functions appearing in the analysis of the nominal-group are the Numerative (a quantifier), the Deictic (usually a determiner), and the Head (often a noun, pronoun, substitute etc., but may be conflated with either of the other two functions):

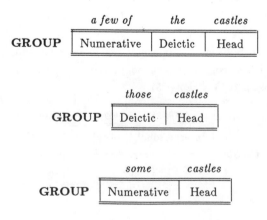

	a few of	*the*	*castles*
GROUP	Numerative	Deictic	Head

	those	*castles*
GROUP	Deictic	Head

	some	*castles*
GROUP	Numerative	Head

	(I'll take)	*a few of*	*those*
GROUP		Numerative	Deictic
			Head

3.3.6. Rank

Although the emphasis in systemic grammar is primarily on the functional issues of language, it still must relate this function to structure. This requires a structural analysis that is similar to that found in the traditional "immediate constituent" grammars, but that is also consistent with *all* of the different functional analyses. The deep, narrow trees (where each node has a small number of constituents) produced by immediate constituent grammars typically will conflict with at least one of the functional analyses.

Systemic grammar therefore adopts an approach called "minimal bracketing" (where constituents are grouped together in a separate level of structure only when absolutely necessary, see deJoia and Stenton, 1980, §3). In fact there are only a small, fixed number of groupings called *units*: the "clause-complex," the "clause," the "group"/"phrase," the "word," and the "morpheme." The minimal bracketing of a "rank grammar" has a significant effect on the constituent analysis: the constituent trees are short and bushy rather than long and narrow.

Clearly there is a hierarchical relationship between the various units. The constituents of a clause, for instance, will usually be groups and words, while the constituents of a group will tend to be words. For this reason the relationship between these various units is called *rank*. Since all constituents in systemic grammar are at one of these ranks, systemic grammar is called a "rank grammar" (see deJoia and Stenton, 1980, §608, §609). Note that the top and bottom ranks (clause-complex and morpheme) will not be used in this work.

A constituent normally realized by units at a particular rank may occasionally be realized by a unit of a higher rank. For instance the Deictic in a nominal-group is normally an item at the word rank (e.g. "that" in "that hat"). In the case of a possessive determiner, however, the Deictic may be a nominal-group acting as a word (e.g. *"the elephant's* trunk"). This is called "rankshifting."

It is important to distinguish between "rank" and "delicacy." It is easy to confuse these two scales of abstraction, but in fact they are orthogonal. The feature *nominal-group* is not more delicate than the feature *clause*; they are each the least delicate features at their respective ranks. Starting at the feature *clause*, and increasing in delicacy to *finite* to *indicative* to *interrogative*, the description is not moving toward smaller constituents, but to finer distinctions between classes of clauses.

3.3.7. Realization rules

The features and system networks have been introduced, as have been the ideas of functional analysis and rank. But there is a gap left to be filled between the features and system networks on the one hand, and the functional analysis and constituent structure on the other. This gap is filled by the "realization rules" attached to the features in the grammar.

The realization rules can be regarded as specifying the structural implications of the feature to which they are attached. Elements of structure are represented in realization rules by their function (e.g. Subject, Agent). The set of functions described in §3.3.5 is fairly standard, but unfortunately the realization relationships vary from source to source, and there seems to be no standard notation for even the widely-used ones.

The notation used in this work is taken from (Mann/Halliday). An additional convention of enclosing realization rules in parentheses has been introduced. Some examples of the various realization rules and their associated features will now be presented.

A realization relationship that seems to be used universally in systemic grammars is "conflation" (the symbol is "/" in Mann/Halliday but "=" in Winograd, 1983, p. 305). This states that the same linguistic item realizes more than one function. For instance, the feature *unmarked-declarative-theme* has the realization rule (Subject / Topical), as in "Jack was applauded by the Duke," where "Jack" is functioning as both the Subject and Topical:

	Jack	*was applauded by the Duke*
mood	Subject	
		. . .
theme	Topical	

The "expansion" realization rule takes two arguments: a function to be divided into subfunctions, and one of the subfunctions. For instance, in §3.3.5, Mood was expanded into Subject and Finite—this is written as the two

34

realization rules (Mood(Subject)) and (Mood(Finite)), attached to the features *indicative* and *finite* respectively. Similarly, (Theme(Topical)) is attached to *topical-inserted,* and so on.

Expansion is indicated in the structure diagrams where there are two levels of the same analysis, and one of the functions in the bottom row spans exactly the same distance as two or more functions in the top row. The expansions (Mood(Subject)), (Mood(Finite)), (Residue(Lexverb)), (Residue(Residual)), (Moodtag(Tagfinite)) and (Moodtag(Tagsubject)) are drawn:

	the man	*has*	*eaten*	*the steak*	*has*	*he*
mood	Subject	Finite	Lexverb	Residual	Tagfinite	Tagsubject
	Mood		Residue		Moodtag	

Another realization relationship is "adjacency." This states that the linguistic items realizing two particular functions are adjacent in the structure. Consider the feature *declarative,* which has the realization rule (Subject ˆ Finite), where "ˆ" is the symbol for adjacency. For instance, in "Jack was applauded by the Duke," "Jack" is the Subject, and "was" is the Finite element. The feature *finite* has the realization rule (Mood ˆ Residue). In the same example, which is also *finite,* "Jack was" is the Mood, and "applauded by the Duke" is the Residue.

	Jack	*was*	*applauded by the Duke*
mood	Subject	Finite	
	Mood		Residue

Some other grammars use a realization relation which merely indicates that one of the functions appear after (as opposed to immediately after) the other (e.g. Winograd, 1983, p. 305; Mann et al., 1983). This can be used instead of, or as well as, adjacency.

A special case of adjacency is that in which an item is a leftmost or rightmost constituent, and therefore adjacent to the boundary. The feature *clause* has the realization rule (# ˆ Theme) indicating that in all clauses the Theme is at the beginning. Boundary symbols will be treated here as quasi-functions that appear in adjacency statements like other functions. Mann et al. (1983) have opted to have special realization relationships called "order-at-front" and "order-at-back" which take one real function as an argument. These are simply two notational variants on the same theme.

Since it is convenient to be able to state, for instance, that Subject is the leftmost subfunction of Mood, a new symbol has been introduced to denote the boundary of an expanded function: %. The realization rule (% ˆ Subject) indicates that Subject is the leftmost subfunction of some expanded function. This is not ambiguous since a function can only be a subfunction of at most one function—though it can be associated with other expanded functions by a conflation. For instance Topical is a subfunction only of Theme, and Subject is a subfunction only of Mood, and the Subject and the Topical may be conflated; but there can be no realization rules (Mood(Topical)) or (Theme(Subject)). Expansion, together with conflation, allows very complex structures to be specified. For instance, (Mood(Subject)), (Mood(Finite)), (% ˆ Subject), (Finite ˆ %) (Theme(Interpersonal)), (Theme(Topical)), (% ˆ Interpersonal), (Topical ˆ %), (# ˆ Theme) and (Subject / Topical) constrain the first three items in the clause to be the Interpersonal, the Topical/Subject followed by the Finite:

	perhaps	*this teapot*	*was*	. . .
mood		Subject	Finite	
		Mood		
theme	Interpersonal	Topical		
	Theme			

The grammar may require a function to be realized by a particular lexical item. This is indicated by the realization relationship "lexify," and denoted by the symbol "=". This is most often found at the word rank, but is also found at the clause and group ranks.

In fact lexify is not used in the clause network (Mann/Halliday) but was adopted from Mann et al. (e.g. 1983, p. 25) for convenience. For instance the feature *speaker-subject* was given the realization rule (Subject = I) as in:

	I	*like*	*that*
mood	Subject		

A realization rule that is particularly important in this work is "preselection" (the symbol ":" is used in Mann/Halliday, but it is called "classification" with the symbol "/" in Winograd, 1983, p. 305). This is the form of realization used to interface the different system networks. Sometimes classification at the clause rank, for instance, implies classification for its constituents at other ranks. A preselection classifies a linguistic item (identified by a function) by selecting a feature for that item from a network representing a lower level of classification. For instance, the feature *speaker-subject* mentioned above has the realization rules (Finite : !first-person) and (Finite : !v-singular) which preselect, from the verb network at the word rank, the features classifying the Finite as a first person singular verb. The grammar described in Mann et al. (1983) uses the symbol "!" instead of ":" when preselecting lexical features because that grammar has no networks at the word rank (e.g. (Finite ! pastform) ibid., p. 45). Even though the grammar used here does have word rank networks, it is useful to distinguish preselections from the word rank to avoid confusion where it is not clear to which rank a feature belongs (e.g. it may not be clear if the feature name *singular* has been used in the nominal-group network or the noun network). Thus in the grammar described throughout the present work, the symbol ":" is used for all preselections, but features at the word rank are prefixed with a "!" (*!singular* as opposed to *singular*). This is purely a notational convention to aid the reader; there is no linguistic or computational significance.

This (Function : feature) notation is fine so long as the feature applies to the constituent immediately below that represented by the function in the constituent tree. In the case of Finite, it is realized by a verb so there is no problem preselecting the verb features *!first-person* and *!v-singular*.

However, consider the case of the feature *proper-subject* in the clause network (Mann/Halliday). The problem is that the Subject will be realized by a nominal-group, and what is really needed is for the feature *!proper* to be preselected for the Head of that nominal-group—not for the nominal-group itself. There appears to be no suitable notation currently in the systemic literature. Of course it is possible to introduce a special feature (e.g. *proper*) at the group rank which itself has the realization rule (Head : !proper). This intermediate feature addition has been avoided here by using a "path notation" for preselection

37

realization rules. Instead of just giving the single function, a whole *path* of functions are specified, separated by the symbol "<" (symbolizing the constituent tree). The feature *proper-subject* has the realization rule (Subject<Head : !proper).

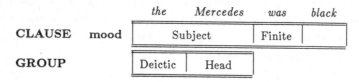

Here the group analysis of the Subject is included in the diagram.

Paths can easily be represented with, and read from, a structure diagram. For instance, in the clause "Jack's uncle's hat was mashed", there are several embedded groups (as shown below):

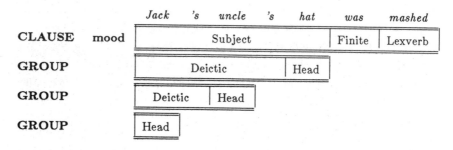

Jack's uncle's hat	is the Subject
Jack's uncle's	is the Subject<Deictic
Jack's	is the Subject<Deictic<Deictic
Jack	is the Subject<Deictic<Deictic<Head
uncle	is the Subject<Deictic<Head
hat	is the Subject<Head

One type of realization rule which is almost universal in the systemic literature but *not* used here is "insertion" (Mann et al., 1983, p. 25), also called "inclusion" (Winograd, 1983, p. 305), and represented by the symbol "+". For instance, the feature *finite* (Mann/Halliday) has the realization rule (+ Finite) meaning that finite clauses have Finite elements. The feature *determined* in a nominal-group network may have the realization rule (+ Deictic) meaning that determined nominal-groups have an element functioning as Deictic.

This type of realization rule has not been implemented here because in any grammar detailed enough to be used in an automatic text-generation system, the functions that are inserted will always appear in other realization relationships (at least when given the set of relationships outlined above). Therefore the insertion statements are at least technically redundant. It could perhaps be argued that it is useful to provide insertion statements for linguistic clarity, but the author's experience has not indicated this (e.g. Note in Winograd, 1983, p. 305 that inclusion is almost always combined with another realization relationship in the same rule).

3.3.8. The metafunctions

Following Malinowski's observation that language functions can be grouped into abstract categories, Halliday has identified three general "metafunctions" in adult language. [1]

The "ideational" metafunction is language functioning to represent the "world" in general—processes, events, actions, objects etc., as well as logical relationships between them (Halliday, 1978, p. 21).

The "interpersonal" metafunction is language functioning to express roles of the speaker in the discourse. The speaker is communicating: what is being talked about, the relationship with the hearer (e.g. contradicting, supporting), how strongly the text is believed, whether or not the speaker is happy about what is being said, and so on (ibid.).

The "textual" metafunction of language is to organize the text in such a way that it is internally cohesive, and fits into both the larger discourse and the social situation in general. In other words it ensures that the text is relevant and coherent (ibid.).

Although the metafunctions can be correlated with the different functional analyses, in keeping with the spirit of systemic grammar the metafunctions have their basis in the paradigmatic description. Looking at system networks of natural languages, Halliday noted that there tends to be a high degree of interdependence among some groups of features and relatively low interdependence between these groups. The groups of features correspond to the three metafunctions mentioned above.

> In origin ..., the concept of metafunction is an empirical claim about the paradigmatic organization of the clause systems in English. (Martin, 1984)

Halliday claims (1978, pp. 21-2) that these metafunctions are common to all adult natural language (not just English). Presumably other languages may have others, such as the "magical" metafunction observed by Malinowski in the Polynesian languages he encountered.

The functional analyses presented above are correlated with the three metafunctions. The realization rules attached to ideational features in general specify the transitivity and ergativity analyses, the realization rules attached to interpersonal features in general specify the analysis of mood (as illustrated by Figure 3.4), and the realization rules attached to textual features in general specify the theme analysis.

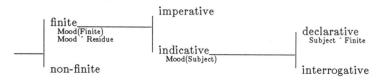

Figure 3.4. Some interpersonal systems.

The relationship between function and metafunction can perhaps best be illustrated through an analogy with biology.

> A simple structural analysis would be based on laying out maps of organs, what they connected to, and what tissue structures appeared in which areas. A functional analysis would involve a study of physiology, viewing the body as an intertwined set of systems (such as the circulatory system and the respiratory system) and describing individual organs and internal structures in terms of the functions they serve in each of these systems. A macro-functional analysis would include an understanding of the functions these systems serve in preserving the individual and the species. The organs and structures can be described in terms of the way they contribute to one or more of the necessary macro-functions (which have been succinctly characterized as 'feeding, fleeing, and reproduction'). (Winograd, 1983, p. 288)

A simple structural (syntagmatic) analysis in linguistics would be based on laying out maps of constituents, what they are adjacent to, and what constituents appear in which places in the string. A functional analysis would involve viewing the text as intertwined sets of syntactic functions (such as Agent, Process, Goal; Subject, Finite; Theme, Rheme) and describing individual constituents in terms of the functions they serve in each of these. A macro-functional analysis—Halliday now uses the term *metafunctional* for adults—would include an understanding of the functions these sets of syntactic functions serve in communication. The constituents and structures can be described in terms of the way they contribute to one or more of the necessary metafunctions (which have been succinctly characterized as "ideational, interpersonal, and textual."

3.3.9. Recursive systems

The multidimensional functional analysis and the principle of minimal bracketing have led to a serious problem with the system network notation. The advantages of minimal bracketing are often illustrated using the example of "parataxis." Parataxis is simply a logical combination of items of the same rank forming a list (see Halliday and Martin, 1981, Glossary—e.g. "John and Bill and Mary," "the red one, the blue one, or the black one," this list of examples and so on). The minimal bracketing principle says that paratactic structure should be flat:

Whereas immediate constituent grammars would form the list recursively, resulting in a tree:

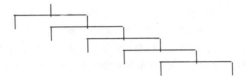

Since the paratactic lists can be arbitrarily long, *some* recursive mechanism is needed to produce the structure. The solution suggested in the current systemic literature is the "recursive system," which amounts to a loop in the system network. E.g.:

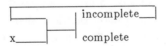

Hudson (1971, pp. 61-2) claims:

> The big advantage of allowing recursion of this kind in the system network, rather than in rules that affect the structure directly, is that it does not add unwarranted structure. If we use a phrase-structure rule, such as 'x → x+x' then we can generate nothing but binary structures,

41

whereas we really want to generate single layers of structure with any number of ICs. In TG theory, the way has been found out of this dilemma by the introduction of a new bit of theoretical apparatus, the 'rule schema', but in systemic theory, no special apparatus is needed. We allow 'incomplete' to occur any number of times in the paradigmatic description of an item, by a recursive system, and then we map each occurrence of 'incomplete' onto a separate element in the item's structure.

Despite Hudson's claims, it is readily apparent that there are some problems with recursive systems. If features are the name of a class, then the distinction made here involves the number of times an item belongs to a particular class, which makes little sense. Hudson proposes to abolish the one-to-one correspondence between classes and features. This not only introduces new theoretical problems, but also does not really solve the original problem. For instance, feature x in the example is really only an entry condition for the first occurrence of the choice—not those following—yet the entry condition in the network is always a disjunction involving x. More seriously, the functions in the realization rules inside the loop would need to be indexed (as Halliday and Martin, 1981, Glossary, say they are), and almost certainly require variables (e.g. $(Fn \,\hat{} \, Fn+1)$).

Given the problems with recursive systems, it is not surprising that they have not been implemented in previous text generation projects (e.g. Davey, 1978, says he is not convinced that recursive systems are the answer to the problem).

There are some general approaches that might lead to a satisfactory solution. All of these retain the one-to-one correspondence between features and classes. First, since it appears that even following Hudson's radical proposal the functions would have to be indexed, the result ends up looking very much like a schema anyway. Perhaps it would be best just to remove the recursive entry condition and treat features with indexed functions as schemas of some sort.

The suggestion in McCord (1975) is that new realization relations could be introduced that operate uniformly on lists of structure nodes. For instance there could be a realization relation "listify" that is similar to "lexify" but associates a list of lexical items with a function. The problem here is that paratactic elements (for example) may not always be treated uniformly (e.g. "John, Bill, *and* Mary"). This suggestion has the advantage of not requiring an entirely new mechanism to be added to systemic grammar, but it is not clear that it will be sufficient in all cases.

There is no doubt that a replacement needs to be found for recursive systems. This is a major theoretical problem that severely restricts the abilities of systemic text generators. Nevertheless, no attempt has been made to remedy this situation here; system networks are required to be loop-free and parataxis has been avoided.

3.4. The strata

Halliday adopts

> ... the general perspective on the linguistic system you find in Hjelmslev, in the Prague school, with Firth in the London school, with Lamb, and to a certain extent with Pike—language as a basically tristratal system: semantics, grammar, phonology. (Halliday, 1978, p. 39)

It should be pointed out that "grammar" here refers to lexicogrammar, i.e. it includes vocabulary. Also, "phonology" should really be expanded to "phonology/orthography" to include writing as well as speaking (as Halliday often does elsewhere in his writings).

It is important to understand that the relationship between these strata is not one of delicacy; for instance, phonology is not just a more detailed continuation of the grammar. Each stratum has its own relationships and dimensions of abstraction—this is the point of stratification. Semantics, grammar and phonology are each described in terms most appropriate to that particular aspect of language. The result is three different but not independent representations of language.

Although the three strata are different representations, the *representation language* for the most part is the same. Each description is organized as systems of features. As stressed earlier, this means that the representation at each of the strata is a description of "potential."

3.4.1. The semantic stratum

The semantic stratum is a representation of the speaker's "meaning potential": using Halliday's gloss, this is what a speaker "can mean." For instance, suppose a mother wants to control the behaviour of her child by issuing a threat. There are two potential choices: she may threaten the child's privileges, or she may threaten some form of physical punishment. The semantic stratum will be discussed in detail in §3.5 and §3.6.

3.4.2. The grammatical stratum

The grammatical stratum is a representation of what the speaker "can say" (in the sense of "formulate"). A typical choice here is between an *indicative* and an *imperative* clause. The grammatical stratum has already been discussed in some detail in this chapter.

3.4.3. The phonological/orthographic stratum

The phonological/orthographic stratum is a representation of how the speaker "can sound" or "can write." Typical kinds of choices here are whether or not to emphasize a particular word in the case of phonology, or what punctuation to use in orthography. This stratum will not be discussed further because it follows the same theoretical principles as the other two strata, and has not been implemented.

3.4.4. Interstratal preselection

Although the strata have been presented as different representations, they are clearly related. The relationships are represented through interstratal preselection, which is essentially the same as the preselection between ranks described earlier. Features at the semantic stratum may have realization rules which preselect grammatical features. Similarly, grammatical features may preselect features from the phonological/orthographic stratum. As Halliday (1973, p. 85) says:

> In general the options in a semantic network will be realized by selections of features in the grammar—rather than 'bypassing' the grammatical systems and finding direct expression as formal items.

Thus, sets of features at the semantic stratum are mapped, using preselection, onto sets of features at the grammatical stratum which are, in turn, mapped onto sets of features at the phonological/orthographic stratum. At the phonological/orthographic stratum there is no lower stratum from which to preselect, so the realization is in terms of physical characteristics instead of features.

Note that there is no restriction on the *rank* from which grammatical features are preselected. The semantics can, and in most grammars probably must, preselect some features from each of the clause, group and word ranks. This means that the path of preselections from the semantics to the word rank can involve several steps. For instance, in the case of the Subject, the number is important at the clause rank, so the semantics may preselect the feature *singular-subject.* One of the realization rules of this feature preselects the feature *singular* from the nominal-group network. This in turn results in the feature *!singular* being preselected from the noun network (for the Head function). In other cases, for instance to preselect a lexical entry like *!floor,* the semantic stratum preselects the feature directly from the word rank. In other cases the semantic stratum chooses from the nominal-group network—for instance, to preselect features like *non-possessive-nom,* which preselects the feature *!non-possessive* for the Head. It makes no difference what the preselection path is. For instance all the above features at the word rank are entry conditions to a gate:

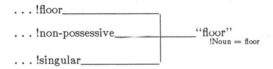

Since there is no phonological/orthographic stratum, the "lexify" realization rule above simply associates a lexical item with the function.

3.5. The semantic stratum

The semantic stratum, as it appears in the systemic theory, is particularly relevant to systemic work on text generation. This is because the semantic stratum must act as the interface between the extralinguistic inference and the grammar. Although systemic grammar has been used in several text-generation projects, the semantic stratum as described in (Halliday, 1978) has never been included. For these reasons the semantic stratum will be given some extra attention here.

The term "semantic" in systemic theory has quite different connotations than it does in other branches of linguistics. In systemic linguistics "semantics" includes much of what is normally referred to as "pragmatics," and it is not represented or defined in terms of truth functions. Semantics here is directly related to Malinowski's notion of "context of situation." In fact Halliday originally used the term "contextual" to refer to this stratum.

> *All* language functions in contexts of situation, and is relatable to those contexts. The question is not what peculiarities of vocabulary, or grammar or pronunciation, can be directly accounted for by reference to the situation. It is *which* kinds of situational factor determine *which* kinds

of selection in the linguistic system. (Halliday, 1978, p. 32)

Thus, in systemic theory, the context becomes the key to the semantics. Clearly, in this case a more precise notion of "context" is required. To this end Halliday and others have developed the idea of "register."

> Types of linguistic situation differ from one another, broadly speaking, in three respects: first, what is actually taking place; secondly, who is taking part; and thirdly, what part language is playing. These three variables, taken together determine the range within which meanings are selected and the forms which are used for their expressions. In other words, they determine the 'register'.
>
> The notion of register is at once very simple and very powerful. It refers to the fact that the language we speak or write varies according to the type of situation. This in itself is no more than stating the obvious. What the theory of register does is to attempt to uncover the general principles which govern this variation, so that we can begin to under-stand *what* situational factors determine *what* linguistic features. (ibid., pp. 31-2).

The three respects in which situations differ, as just described, are termed: *field*—"what is actually taking place"; *tenor*—"who is taking part"; and *mode*— "what part language is playing" (Halliday, 1978, *passim*). Field, tenor and mode are useful conceptual groupings that play a similar role to the metafunctions at the grammatical stratum.

3.5.1. Field
The field is the socially recognized physical setting in which text occurs, including the activities in progress.

3.5.2. Tenor
The tenor is a characterization of the relationship between the participants. This includes not just their respective social positions, discourse roles etc., but also the emotional issues of the moment.

3.5.3. Mode
Mode refers to the role language is playing in a particular situation. This involves characteristics of the text such as whether it is spoken harshly or written, and so on. It also involves the social function the text is performing, e.g. being descriptive, being persuasive etc.

Field, tenor and mode define the register of a social context. The semantic stratum is represented as a system network that specifies the choices available in field, tenor and mode—i.e. it is a paradigmatic description of register.

3.5.4. Register and metafunction

Halliday (ibid.) relates field, tenor and mode individually and as a group to the metafunctions at the grammatical stratum (see Section §3.3.8). Both register and metafunction provide broad organizational principles to explain the relationship between features or sets of features at their respective strata. Individually, field is related to the ideational metafunction, by stating the general principle that semantic features associated with field tend to preselect ideational features. Tenor and the interpersonal metafunction have the same relationship, as do mode and the textual metafunction.

As an illustration, Halliday briefly describes two registers as follows (ibid., p. 226 and p. 115 respectively):

Field: Instruction: the instruction of a novice
- in a board game (e.g. Monopoly) with equipment present
- for the purpose of enabling him to participate

Tenor: Equal and intimate: three young adult males; acquainted
- but with hierarchy in the situation (2 experts, 1 novice)
- leading to superior-inferior role relationships

Mode: Spoken: unrehearsed Didactic and explanatory, with undertone of non-seriousness
- with feedback: question-and-answer, correction of error

Field Child at play: manipulating movable objects (wheeled vehicles) with related fixtures, assisted by adult; concurrently associating (i) similar past events, (ii) similar absent objects; also evaluating objects in terms of each other and of processes.

Tenor Small child and parent interacting: child determining course of action, (i) announcing his own intentions, (ii) controlling actions of parent; concurrently sharing and seeking corroboration of own experience with parent.

Mode Spoken, alternately monologue and dialogue, task-oriented; pragmatic, (i) referring to processes and objects of situation, (ii) relating to and furthering child's own actions, (iii) demanding other objects; interposed with narrative and exploratory elements.

Here are some examples of interactions between register and the grammar: In the second example, when assistance from the adult is the subject matter, the ideational features related to benefaction are relevant to the field. Similarly, when similar events are recalled, the ideational feature *past* will be preselected. In the case of tenor, interaction with the parent will require preselecting the interpersonal features concerning "person." Determination of course of events will mean preselecting interpersonal mood and polarity features. In the case of mode, reference to objects and situations will involve anaphoric and exophoric reference by preselecting textual features (ibid., p. 117).

3.5.5. A closer look

Unfortunately, there has been little detailed work done on the semantic stratum, and several important issues are yet to be resolved.

For instance, one of the most important aspects of the grammatical stratum is the specification of grammatical structure. Halliday (1978, p. 41) admits:

> We know more or less what the nature of grammatical structure is. We know that constituent structure in some form or other is an adequate form of representation of the structures [at] the lexicogrammatical level. It is much less clear what is the nature of the structures [at] the semantic level.... [When working with the language of young children] it has been possible to bypass the level of semantic structure and go straight into lexicogrammatical constituent structure. That's all right for certain limited purposes. But there is obviously a limitation here, and when we attempt semantic representation for anything other than these highly restricted fields, it is almost certainly going to be necessary to build in some concept of semantic structure. But what it will look like exactly I don't know. I don't think we can tell yet.

For reasons of convenience, and since it seems to be adequate for the limited examples presented here, the realization rules at the grammatical stratum have been used at the semantic stratum as well. In other words, a simplifying assumption has been made that the structures at the semantic stratum are directly analogous to the structures at the grammatical stratum. This implies that there are semantic functions analogous to Agent, Subject etc.

3.6. Example

An example of the semantic stratum for a typical expert system domain would be ideal at this point, but unfortunately the only example from adult registers that Halliday presents in any detail is that of a mother threatening her child. Nevertheless, this will be sufficient to illustrate the ideas discussed in the previous section.

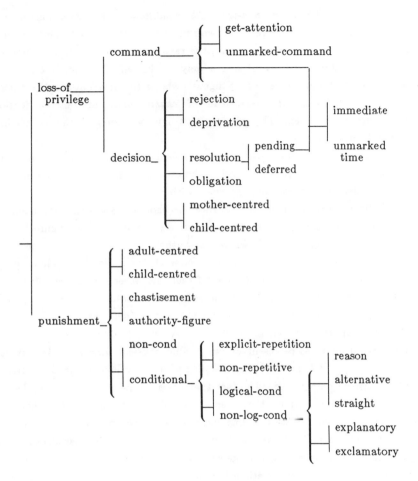

Figure 3.5. Some semantic choices.

Figure 3.5 shows some systems from a semantic system network—the gates and realization rules have been omitted.

Note that this network represents only some of the choices for some very restricted registers. The choices illustrated here are mainly to do with tenor—the specific relationship between the mother and her child. For instance, in the case of *explanatory* on one hand, the mother is acting as an informant and backing it up with a threat; in the case of *exclamatory* on the other hand, the mother is setting herself up as the authority and telling what the consequences of disobedience will be. For instance, if the features *straight, explicit-repetition,*

49

chastisement, adult-centred, non-log-cond, conditional, and *punishment* are chosen with *explanatory,* the result is "you mustn't do that, next time I'll smack you". If *exclamatory* is chosen instead, the text is "don't do that, next time I'll smack you". Alternatively, the mother may set herself up as an intermediary between the child and an "authority figure" who is to carry out the threatened action. For instance, suppose instead of *chastisement* above, the feature *authority-figure* is chosen. The resulting text may be "don't do that, next time Daddy will smack you".

When generating a clause, the choices for field and mode must also be made. The mode will almost certainly involve choosing a harsh tone of speech. The choices for field and mode may interact with the choices illustrated here for tenor. Field choices are likely to influence the choice of authority figure should the tenor require one. If the scene is set at home, the authority figure is very likely to be the father. If set elsewhere, the authority figure may be, for instance, a policeman (Halliday, 1978, p. 84). Of course the field may also influence the mode—the tone of voice may be lowered if there are other people present, and so on. Thus there may be a gate for a mode feature *harsh-whisper* that has entry conditions from both the field and tenor sections of the network.

It may appear that semantic features like *people-nearby* imply that the semantic stratum must represent every possible physical situation. This is *not* the case—only those factors that are linguistically relevant for a particular speaker must be represented. The fact that there are people nearby may have a significant effect on the form the utterance should take; the fact that there is a person in the Empire State Building wearing red socks may not. The point is that there is a discernible set of factors which, for a particular speaker, are linguistically relevant during text generation. The semantic stratum represents these and their various interrelationships.

3.7. Summary

The purpose of this chapter has been to introduce and motivate those concepts from systemic linguistics that play a significant role in the rest of the work. The origin of many of these concepts can be traced back through Halliday, through Firth and Hjelmslev, to Malinowski. Description of the functions and metafunctions of language, first observed by Malinowski, is facilitated by the paradigmatic and realizational descriptions of Firth and Hjelmslev respectively. Malinowski's emphasis on the social and cultural environment of language led to Firth's notion of the "multiplicity of languages" within a language, and to Halliday's work on register and the semantic stratum.

The goals of systemic grammar were then discussed. The primary goal of systemic grammar was identified as functional description, supported by the goal of classification. It was argued that the goal of functional description is complementary to the traditional linguistic goal of structural or syntagmatic description, in the same way as physiology and anatomy are complementary in biology.

Some specific concepts from systemic grammar were then discussed, and illustrated at the grammatical stratum. It was then pointed out that there are in fact three strata: the semantic, the grammatical, and the phonological/orthographic. Since the preceding discussions were primarily concerned with the grammatical stratum, and since the semantic stratum plays a particularly important role in the approach to text generation described later, the semantic stratum was then discussed in some detail.

4
The conflation

Slang ... is often used by people who are deliberately
adopting a certain speech variant for social purposes.
(Halliday, 1978, p. 158)

The previous two chapters have discussed the independent fields of AI problem solving and systemic grammar. This chapter will point out that in fact there is an important relationship between the two fields that can form the basis for a "Systemic Linguistic Approach to Natural-language Generation" (SLANG). The first few sections will describe the various facets of the relationship between AI problem solving and systemic grammar, and the text-generation method that results. Then some examples will be presented to illustrate the text-generation method just described. Finally there will be a short discussion of the metatheoretical aspects of this approach to text generation.

4.1. The fundamental relationship

> The central nature of intelligent problem solving is that a system must construct its solution selectively and efficiently from a space of alternatives. (Hayes-Roth et al., 1983a, p. 20)

> We shall define language as 'meaning potential': that is, as sets of options, or alternatives, in meaning, that are available to the speaker-hearer. (Halliday in deJoia and Stenton, 1980, §572)

Compare these two quotations. The fields of study examined in the previous two chapters are both organized around a space of alternatives. Notice that these passages do not refer to peripheral issues; the first few words of each, "The central nature of intelligent problem solving is ..." and "We shall define language as ...," indicate that the issues involving alternatives lie at the nucleus of the respective disciplines. This being the case, there is clearly a *fundamental relationship* between AI problem solving and systemic grammar. This section will probe into this fundamental relationship, in an attempt to discover its origins and nature.

4.1.1. Alternatives in AI problem solving

AI problem solving is characterized as a "search" through a space of alternatives. Chapter 2 discussed some of the techniques employed by AI problem solvers over the years to find a solution within a space of alternatives. The techniques ranged from blindly searching through the possibilities until a solution was found, to efficient goal-directed knowledge-based techniques that selectively considered only alternatives that may lead to a solution. Whether the alternatives are explicitly searched or whether they are avoided, the entire space of alternatives is always at least implicitly represented.

4.1.2. Alternatives in systemic linguistics

The emphasis on alternatives in systemic linguistics originated in two separate aspects of Malinowski's work (e.g. 1923). He characterized language as an action, an integral part of the everyday actions in a society. He also argued that language can only be understood in a specific context. The second point was developed later by Firth when he precisely stated, and indeed defined, the context of language in terms of "potential":

> ... Firth built his linguistic theory around the original and fundamental concept of the 'system', as used by him in a technical sense; and this is precisely a means of describing the potential, and of relating the actual to it....
>
> The potential of language is a meaning potential. This meaning potential is the linguistic realization of the behaviour potential; 'can mean' is 'can do' when translated into language. The meaning potential is in turn realized in the language system as lexico-grammatical potential, which is what the speaker 'can say'. (Halliday, 1973, pp. 50-1)

Thus in systemic linguistics, the starting point is the set of alternatives in meaning. Linguistic contexts are characterized by the alternatives in meaning available in the particular context—meaning potential. These alternatives are realized by, or mapped onto, sets of grammatical alternatives.

One important point also apparent from the quotation is that systemic theory treats extralinguistic matters in terms of potential as well. An agent in a particular (social rather than linguistic) context has a "behaviour potential"—what the agent "can do." Some of the alternatives in social situations are linguistic, and these form the meaning potential. The crucial point is that the linguistic *alternatives* are just a subset of the behavioural *alternatives* that can realize the behavioural potential.

Now it must be understood that the notion of alternatives—paradigmatic description—plays a more central role in systemic grammar than in other linguistic theories:

> If we go back to the Hjelmslevian (originally Saussurean) distinction of paradigmatic and syntagmatic, most of modern linguistic theory has given priority to the syntagmatic form of organization. *Structure* means (abstract) *constituency,* which is a syntagmatic concept. Lamb treats the two axes together: for him a linguistic stratum is a network embodying both syntagmatic and paradigmatic relations all mixed up together, in patterns of what he calls AND and OR nodes. I take out the paradigmatic relations (Firth's *system)* and give priority to these; for me the underlying organization at each level is paradigmatic. (Halliday, 1978, p. 40)

In Halliday's theory, the alternatives are dependent on other alternatives, not on structures:

> ... and here I depart from Firth, for whom the environment of a system was a place in structure—the entry condition was syntagmatic, whereas mine is again paradigmatic. (ibid., p. 41)

The important point to note here is that while many grammatical theories have alternatives as a (perhaps even an important) consideration, they are usually first and foremost theories of structure, and the representation of alternatives is sacrificed to this end. Whereas in systemic grammar the alternatives are primary.

> By 'text', then, we understand a continuous process of semantic choice. Text is meaning and meaning is choice, an ongoing current of selections each in its paradigmatic environment of what *might have* been meant (but was not). It is the paradigmatic environment—the innumerable subsystems that make up the semantic system—that must provide the basis of the description, if the text is to be related to higher orders of meaning, whether social, literary, or of some other semiotic universe. (ibid., p.137)

Thus in systemic linguistics, paradigmatic description—description in terms of alternatives—is the crucial representational concern.

4.1.3. The fountainhead

Noting the fact that AI problem solving and systemic grammar are both organized around alternatives is only the first step. Next it must be noted that in knowledge-based AI problem solving, the alternatives represent the problem—

knowledge about the alternatives is then required to guide the problem solver to a solution. Systemic grammar is knowledge about linguistic alternatives; the entry condition and realization rules specify the conditions and effects of a particular alternative—exactly the information required by an AI problem solver. Thus the *primum mobile* of this work becomes apparent: a systemic grammar can be interpreted as linguistic problem-solving knowledge and used by an AI problem solver to find—selectively and efficiently—the solution to linguistic problems in exactly the same way as knowledge from other domains is used to solve problems in those domains.

4.2. The conflation

A particularly important consequence of the fundamental relationship between AI problem solving and systemic grammar is that the central representations found in each of the two fields are equivalent. This means that a systemic grammar can be directly interpreted as both linguistic description and problem-solving knowledge simultaneously—i.e. the two interpretations can be conflated. This conflation provides the impetus for a new approach to text generation, but is only the beginning. The conflation reaches much further than just the surface representation; it extends to the foundations of systemic theory.

The discussion here, and throughout the remainder of the book, will involve describing the relationship between systemic grammar and one particular variation of the AI representation: production rules (see §2.1). A production system is only one of several architectures able to selectively and efficiently process a space of alternatives. Production rules were chosen here for reasons of simplicity, accessibility and for their formal properties (see Chapter 5). It is important that the reader understand that similar expositions could be given for representations such as "objects" (see §6.5).

Since both problem-solving knowledge and systemic grammar must describe the complex relationships between interdependent alternatives, it is not too surprising that they developed the same basic representations. For each alternative, the conditions under which the alternative is applicable must be represented, as must the effects or consequences of the particular alternative. Both AI problem solving and systemic grammar have adopted this two-part representation.

4.2.1. Conflating gates and forward-chaining rules

Notice that gates, as described in Chapter 3, are represented in terms of conditions and effects. Gates have a set of entry conditions and a set of realization rules. Consider the gate feature *does* represented in Figure 4.1 in systemic notation.

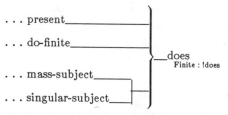

Figure 4.1. A gate (Mann/Halliday).

If the features *present* and *do-finite* have been selected, and either *mass-subject* or *singular-subject* has been selected, then the feature *does* must be selected. The effect or consequence of choosing this feature is that the lexical feature *!does* is preselected, so the Finite element will be realized by one of "does", "doesn't" or "does not".

Now, since production rules, an AI problem-solving representation, also have conditions and effects, gates can be interpreted as production rules. E.g.:

    if   *present* and *do-finite*
          and one of *singular-subject* or *mass-subject*
          have been chosen,
    then choose *does* and preselect the lexical feature *!does* for the Finite.

This can be used for simple forward-chaining as described in Chapter 2. Interpreting entry conditions of a gate as the LHS of a production rule, and the choice and realizations as the RHS, corresponds to the intuitive interpretation of a gate: if the logical combination of features acting as the entry condition to a gate feature is satisfied, then choose the feature and constrain/modify the structure of the text according to the realization rules.

Thus we can interpret a gate in any of these representations (system network, or the various production notations, e.g. see Chapter 6 for the OPS5 representation) either as a piece of a systemic grammar, or as a piece of problem-solving knowledge. In fact it is advantageous to conflate these interpretations—make *both* interpretations simultaneously.

4.2.2. Conflating systems and backward-chaining rules

Suppose the features in a system network that are terms in a system are interpreted similarly. For every feature in a system there will be one rule stating:

> if   the entry conditions of the system are satisfied,
> then choose this feature and perform the actions
>   specified by the realization rules.

Notice that if these rules are interpreted as forward-chaining rules, they are not much use to the problem solver, since there will be several such rules for any particular system, and the problem solver has no way to choose between them. Specifying in the representation that the terms in a system are mutually exclusive doesn't help. The technique of backward-chaining will be used instead. If there is a goal to choose the feature or a goal that can be satisfied by the realization rules, then this production can be used to achieve the goal, and the entry conditions will be set as subgoals.

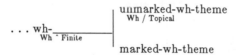

Figure 4.2. A system (Mann/Halliday).

The feature *unmarked-wh-theme* can be interpreted as a backward-chaining rule: if there is a goal to choose *unmarked-wh-theme* or to conflate the Topical with the Wh element, then choose *unmarked-wh-theme*, conflate the Topical with the Wh element, and set a subgoal to choose *wh-*. Again this rule could be written in any of the various production notations as well as the system network notation.

4.2.3. Conflating the grammar and the knowledge base

Thus all the features in a systemic grammar, together with their entry conditions and realization rules, whether they form gates or systems, can be interpreted as problem-solving rules of the kind used by AI problem solvers. This means that the grammatical stratum as a whole can be interpreted as a knowledge base (more likely part of a larger knowledge base) of grammatical knowledge. This knowledge (as will be seen in the next section) can be used to solve grammatical problems in exactly the same way as medical knowledge can be used to solve medical problems, and chemistry knowledge can be used to solve chemistry problems.

4.2.4. Conflating text generation with problem solving

Having shown that the fundamental relationship between systemic grammar and AI problem solving allows the systemic *representation* to be interpreted both as a grammar and as problem-solving knowledge, it will now be possible to show that the process of systemic text generation can be conflated with the process of problem solving.

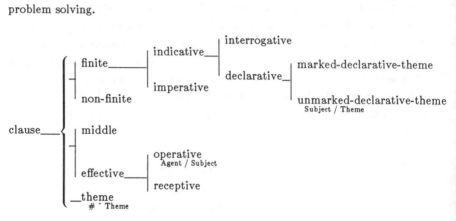

Figure 4.3. A grammar excerpt.

Consider the simplified systemic fragment in Figure 4.3, and imagine a hypothetical problem solver that can perform forward- and backward-chaining. Suppose the semantics sets the goal to conflate the Agent and the Theme. This is a grammatical problem that can be solved using the grammatical knowledge contained in the grammar. This goal cannot be solved immediately since no feature has a realization rule conflating these two functions. However, assuming there is a general rule expressing the transitivity of conflation, this rule can set as subgoals: the conflation of the Agent with X, and the conflation of the X with the Theme—where X can be instantiated to Subject. The features *operative* and *unmarked-declarative-theme* respectively have these realization rules (effects) so the backward-chaining begins there.

The feature *operative,* to start with, has the entry condition *effective*. So *effective* becomes a subgoal. It in turn has the entry condition *clause* which then becomes a subgoal. This chain of reasoning stops once *clause* is chosen because it has no entry conditions. Similarly, the problem solver will backward-chain from *unmarked-declarative-theme* through *declarative, indicative, finite* and *clause*. Note the similarity between "path augmentation" from Mann et al. (1983, p. 68) and this backward-chaining (but see §7.4 for a comparison).

Sometime after *clause* is chosen in the example, the gate *theme*—interpreted as a forward-chaining rule—will fire, since its entry condition is satisfied. Although this is the only gate in this example, there will be many gates firing like this in a large grammar. The gates may fire in chains because many gates have other gates as their entry conditions.

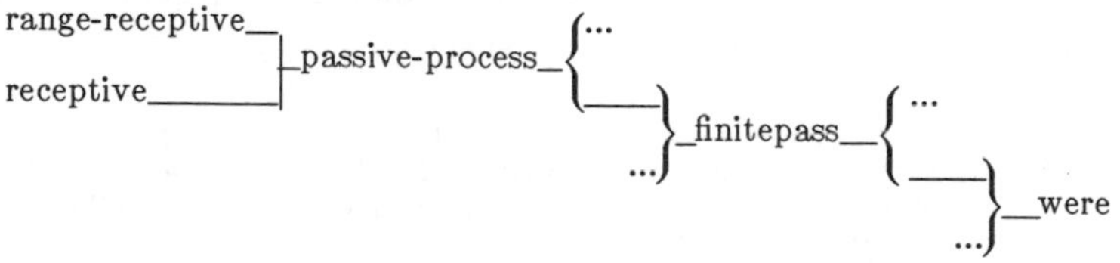

Figure 4.4. A chain of gates from Mann/Halliday.

Figure 4.4 shows a series of gates. If either *range-receptive* or *receptive* (neither of which is a gate) is chosen, *passive-process* fires. One of the gates for which passive process is one of the entry conditions is *finitepass*. One of the gates for which *finitepass* is one of the entry conditions is the gate *were*. Note that there is no choice here, so the input simply propagates through these gate networks like a logic circuit (presumably this is the origin of the term "gate").

It is important to understand that features such as *declarative* and *finite* in the original example, and *finitepass* and *were* in Figure 4.4, have realization rules (not shown here) that become side effects of the solution to the original goal.

Any particular clause, for instance, will involve several goals such as the conflation of the Agent and Topical shown above. After the forward and backward reasoning has been done for each of these goals, and all the realization rules have been processed, the linguistic element will be uniquely determined.

The crux of the matter is that there is no special mechanism here. The problem solver is using grammatical knowledge in exactly the same way as it can use other knowledge in other domains. Thus the process of text generation as described in this section has been conflated with the process of problem solving.

4.2.5. Conflating the semantic stratum with compiled knowledge.
The problem-solving process described in the last section would work. There may, however, be several different ways to achieve any particular goal, some of which

may lead to conflicts with other goals (such as two features being required from the same system) and thus to backtracking (see §2.2.1). This method would have the advantage of being simple; but the disadvantage, of course, is that the backtracking makes even the most common and simple semantic goals very expensive to achieve. AI problem solvers avoid having to solve the same difficult problem repeatedly by "compiling" the result (see §2.3).

It is not a new idea that language involves difficult problems that occur repeatedly and thus is a good candidate for knowledge-compilation techniques. McDonald (1983a, p. 265) says his system cannot do

> ...planning by backwards chaining from desired effects....the effects of such instructions can sometimes be achieved "off-line" however, by having the designer precompute the decision-space that the deliberation would entail and then incorporate it into the component's library as what would in effect be an extension to the rules of the grammar.

Also, as Berwick (Brady and Berwick, 1983, p. 26) says:

> ... it seems hardly likely that every time one hears "Can you pass the salt?" one runs through in toto a long chain of inferences that ends with the conclusion that what was really meant was that someone wants you to pass the salt. The obvious alternative is to squirrel away some commonly occurring deductions ... Of course this approach begs an important research question about the nature and organization of these ...

Berwick's comments clearly apply to generation as well, and the answer to the begged question is Halliday's semantic stratum (as described in §3.5). The nature of the compiled plans or deductions is that they associate grammatical features with situations; their organization is by register. Thus the semantic stratum can be conflated with the high-level compiled knowledge found in AI problem solvers.

Of course the solutions can be compiled to various degrees. For instance any semantic feature that preselects the grammatical feature *unmarked-declarative-theme* in the sample grammar above could also preselect the features *declarative, indicative, finite* and *clause*—thus compiling part of the backward-chaining process described earlier. There appears to be a trade off between clarity and conciseness on one hand, and speed on the other. The approach taken in this work is to have the semantic features preselect only enough grammatical features to determine the result. There are several reasons for this decision. First, in research of this nature clarity is essential. Second, the backward-chaining process is very efficient and does not introduce a large overhead. Third, in the deeply compiled version, making a small change to the grammatical stratum would require many changes to the semantic stratum (unless the compilation is automatic—see §8.3.3).

The question is now: exactly which features need to be preselected to determine the result? The answer lies in the various sources of disjunction in the system network. The major sources of disjunction are the systems. Since features that are terms in systems are interpreted as backward-chaining rules, many of these features will be chosen if and only if they are part of the entry condition of a more delicate feature.

Figure 4.5. Feature dependencies.

Consider Figure 4.5. There is simply no point in preselecting the feature *a*, because then either *b* or *c* must be chosen somehow, and whatever mechanism chooses between them (backward-chaining or preselection) will thereby imply *a*, making the original preselection redundant. Thus it becomes clear that there is no point in preselecting a feature in a system if it is part of the entry condition to another system.

Hudson (1981, p. 214) makes this point when discussing the interface between the grammatical and the phonological strata.

> [T]he only phoneme features that we need to specify as realization for a lexical item are the ones on the right-hand edge of the system-network. This obviously constitutes a major economy in the rules.

The exception to this rule is a result of another form of disjunction: disjunctive entry conditions to systems.

Consider Figure 4.6 (the asterisks indicate unmarkedness and will be referred to in §8.3.2). The features "on the right-hand edge of the system network" i.e. those features that do not have systems to their right are: *lax, centring, non-centring, front, back, I, E* and *A*. Suppose *non-centring* is preselected. At this point the problem solver does not know which of the two disjunctive entry conditions (*tense, peripheral* or both) to set as subgoals, so it cannot continue backward-chaining. On one hand, if the vowel is in fact *peripheral*, then a

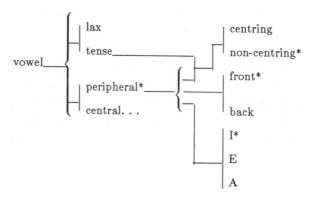

Figure 4.6. Some phonological systems (Hudson, 1981, p. 213).

feature must be preselected from each of the other two systems (*front/back and I/E/A*). In this case *peripheral* will be chosen during the course of backward-chaining from each of these two systems and this gratuitously solves part of the problem with the disjunctive entry condition to *non-centring*. On the other hand, if the vowel is in fact *tense* there is no way to infer this by backward-chaining from other systems, so it must be preselected.

Disjuncts like *peripheral* that are dependent on other systems and not disjunctive with respect to those, are termed "dependent disjuncts." Disjuncts like *tense* that have no such dependents and thus cannot be resolved by backward chaining are termed "independent disjuncts."

Note that gates never need to be preselected. Even if gates have disjunctive entry conditions, it makes no difference because the chaining is in the other direction. Recall Figure 4.1: *mass-subject* and *singular-subject* are disjuncts, but it does not matter which one has been chosen; the rule will still fire.

There is only one difficult case: features that are not terms in systems themselves but are part of the entry conditions to systems. In fact this happens in the Mann/Halliday clause network.

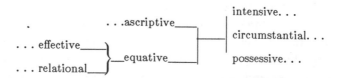

In this fragment *equative* looks like a gate, but in fact must be interpreted as a backward-chaining rule since it may act as the entry condition to a system.

Notice also that it (like *ascriptive*) is an independent disjunct. Therefore the semantics must preselect either *ascriptive* or *equative* if the backward-chaining will run into this disjunction.

The rule then, is that a feature that is a term in a system or is to the left of a system, but does not appear in a purely conjunctive entry condition of another such feature, must be preselected—and is called a "seed feature." All other features can be inferred from seed features (this will be proven in Chapter 5).

The semantic stratum thus acts as a layer of highly-compiled knowledge that guides the problem solving at the grammatical stratum by preselecting seed features. This is illustrated in §4.3 below.

Another topic is the possibility of the problem solver using the grammatical knowledge directly (as in the previous section) in cases where no appropriate compiled/semantic knowledge exists.

> As new, unanticipated patterns crop up, inflexible, compiled solutions fail. General problem-solving abilities allow a more graceful degradation at the outer edges of domain knowledge. (Brachman et al., 1983, p. 46)

It is possible to envisage a text-generation system that when "unanticipated registers crop up" could reason "from first principles" using the knowledge at the grammatical stratum. This will not be taken further here—see §8.3.4.

4.2.6. Conflating behaviour potential and general problem-solving knowledge

It has already been mentioned briefly that systemic theory views "can mean" as one form of "can do"; meaning potential is one form of behavioural potential. This nicely completes the correspondence between AI problem solving and systemic theory, since even the non-linguistic aspects of a problem-solving system can be related to the theory. Consider, for instance, a planning system working with blocks. In a particular situation the planner may have several rules indicating valid actions that can be performed. It makes perfect sense to interpret this as the system's "behaviour potential." Perhaps one of these actions is a linguistic request to another agent to move a block. In this case the behavioural potential is also a meaning potential. The ability to relate linguistic issues to the larger behavioural sphere of activity will prove useful in cases where non-linguistic modes of communication are possible (see Appelt, 1982, 1983, and §7.2.1, §7.3.1).

4.3. An example

Ideally, an example from a typical expert-system application would be given here, but unfortunately the only semantic stratum available is a fragment of a network for a mother threatening her child (described briefly in §3.6). The following example is meant to serve as an analogy to text generation in AI applications.

Suppose there exists a situation involving two agents: a mother and her child. The child has performed some action and the mother, in order to achieve some parental or other social goal, plans to prevent the child from repeating the act. As a result of some reasoning which is not at issue here, the mother decides that solutions such as physically restraining the child and so on would conflict with other goals. Another alternative, however, is to achieve this goal verbally. The task thus becomes a "text planning" task. The mechanism that performs this task is referred to as the "text planner" although it may well be the same general-purpose problem solver working with linguistic knowledge, not necessarily a special-purpose text-planning mechanism.

Again as a result of reasoning which is not at issue here, the text planner decides it can achieve the goal with a two-part utterance: first chastising the child, explaining that the action should not be performed; second threatening punishment if the action is repeated. The text planner reduces the goal of creating this utterance to a set of semantic goals. It is now the job of the text generator to take these semantic goals and produce the natural-language output.

It will be assumed that the text generation is performed using the SLANG approach—a general purpose problem solver uses the knowledge contained in the grammar (semantic and grammatical strata) to generate the text.

To avoid confusion, semantic features are prefixed by "$" to help the reader easily distinguish them from grammatical features (there is no linguistic or computational significance placed on the prefix). Also, where there may be doubt, the network containing a feature will follow the feature in parentheses—e.g. *declarative* (clause).

The semantic goals set by the text planner are: $*straight-threat*, $*explicit-repetition*, $*chastisement*, $*smack*, $*explanatory-cond* and $*adult-centred-punishment*. These semantic goals are seed features of the following excerpt from a semantic stratum to which the text generator has access (Figure 4.7).

The features corresponding to these goals will be chosen and their entry conditions will be set as subgoals. The problem solver backward-chains from $*explanatory-cond* to $*non-logical*, from $*explicit-repetition* to $*conditional*, from $*adult-centred-punishment* to $*punishment*, from $*chastisement* to $*punishment*,

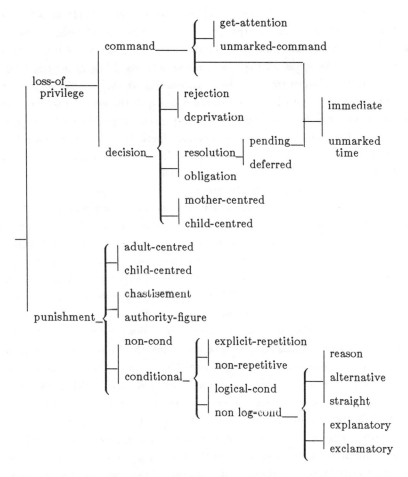

Figure 4.7. (Some feature names have been abbreviated.)

from $non\text{-}logical$ to $conditional$, from $conditional$ to $punishment$, and from $punishment$ to $threat$. Notice that several backward chains often pass through the same goal. The problem solver only achieves the goal once, and if it is set again, it is recognized as being redundant. Sometime during the backward-chaining, some forward-chaining rules (not shown in the above figure, but listed in Appendix C, §C.11) also fire, viz. choosing $explanatory\text{-}cond$ triggers $stated\text{-}cond$, and choosing $explicit\text{-}repetition$ and $straight\text{-}threat$ triggers $repeat\text{-}straight$, while choosing $adult\text{-}centred\text{-}punishment$ and $chastisement$ triggers $mother\text{-}punishes$.

The realization rules of these semantic features (see §C.11) preselect seed features from the grammatical stratum—they set grammatical goals. In fact the problem solver may not wait until all the semantic goals are solved before it begins to solve for goals at the grammatical stratum. The generation will be described word by word from left to right, starting at the top for each word in turn. This is not necessarily the exact order in which the problem solver attacks the goals but in fact is similar to the implemented problem-solving process described in Chapter 6. Many of the details, especially at the grammatical stratum, will be glossed over to make the description comprehensible. Nevertheless, it is hoped that the general idea will be conveyed.

The feature *$conditional* divides the text up into two parts: a condition and a threat, represented by the semantic functions $Cond and $Threat. There is also an adjacency realization rule ($Cond ˆ $Threat) that orders the condition before the threat. This semantic adjacency is not the proper way to do this, but has been used as a shortcut. There should be a clause-complex rank at the grammatical stratum that handles this kind of clause ordering (Halliday, 1985, Chapter 7). So first the generation of the condition will be described.

The feature *$stated-cond* has realization rules which preselect, or set as goals, the features *unmarked-declarative-theme* and *non-attitudinal* (both clause features). The former has the effect of conflating the Topical and the Subject. The feature *$non-logical-cond*, which was inferred from *$explanatory-cond* or *$straight-threat*, sets the goal *non-textual-theme* (clause). When *non-textual-theme* and *non-attitudinal* are chosen, they trigger a forward-chaining rule that together with other inferences orders the Topical at the front of the $Cond clause (by ordering Theme as the leftmost function in the clause, and Topical as the leftmost subfunction of Theme). Since the Topical is conflated with the Subject, this also means that the Subject is at the front of the clause. The feature *$conditional* also sets the grammatical goal *addressee-subject* (clause) which in turn has the effect (Subject = you)[2] and sets the goal *!second-person* (verb) for the Finite. Since the Subject is completely realized, and since it is the first item in the clause, it can now be output. The current structure of the first clause is shown in Figure 4.8.

The feature *$explanatory-cond* sets the goal *modal* (clause), and sets the goal *!must* (verb) for the Modal element.[3] The feature *modal,* chosen to achieve the above goal, has the effect (Modal / Finite). At some point the problem solver backward-chains from *unmarked-declarative-theme* to infer the feature *declarative*, which has the effects (% ˆ Subject), (Finite ˆ %) and (Subject ˆ Finite).

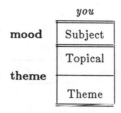

Figure 4.8.

This, together with the fact that Modal and Finite have been conflated, means that the Modal is the next item to be generated. Another of the effects of $non-logical-cond$ is that it sets the goal *unmarked-negative* (clause). At some point the problem solver infers *indicative* and *finite* from *declarative* by backward-chaining. These have the realization rules (Mood(Subject)) and (Residue ˆ #), and (Mood(Finite)) and (Mood ˆ Residue) respectively. From *indicative* and *unmarked-negative* the feature *reduced-negfinite* is inferred by forward-chaining, and sets the goal *!reduced* (verb) for the Finite. The feature *negative* is a condition for *unmarked-negative* and is thus inferred by backward-chaining. This, and the feature *indicative,* result in *negative-finite* being inferred by forward-chaining. The latter feature sets the goal *!negative* for the Finite. When the goals *!negative, !reduced,* and *!must* (all verb) are satisfied by choosing the corresponding features, *"mustn't"* is inferred by the forward-chaining rule shown in Figure 4.9.

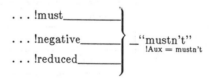

Figure 4.9.

The lexical item "mustn't" thus realizes the Finite/Modal and can now be output (see Figure 4.10).

The realization of the next item to be output, the Process, is again started by the feature $conditional,$ which sets the goal *!-do-* for the Process. This together with *!stem* triggers the feature *"-do-"* which lexifies the verb as "do" (the hyphens distinguish the lexical verb "do" from the auxiliary "do", but both are realized by the same item in the end). The feature *!stem* is inferred as follows: *modal* was an effect of $explanatory-cond;$ *non-past-in* (non-perfective) and *non-*

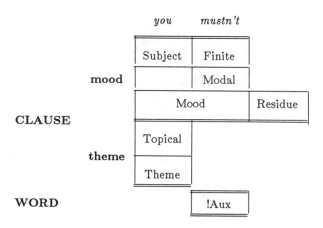

Figure 4.10.

present-in (non-progressive) were both effects of *$conditional*. From these, together with *active-process*, inferred from *operative* by forward-chaining, can be inferred *modalstemlexverb*—which has the effect of setting the goal *!stem* for the Lexverb. However this is also a goal for the Process since the Lexverb and the Process are conflated as an effect of *clause*, which will be inferred at the end of some backward-chaining process. The current relevant structure is shown in Figure 4.11.

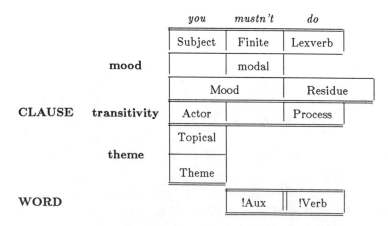

Figure 4.11.

Finally, the grammatical function Goal is generated starting from a number of preselections from the nominal-group network by the semantic feature

$conditional. It sets the following nominal-group goals: *non-possessive-nom, singular, determiner-head* and *far*. The two relevant functions in the nominal-group are the Deictic and the Head, which are conflated in this case by *determiner-head*. The feature *far* has the conditions *demonstrative* and *non-interrogative-det* which are thus inferred by backward-chaining. These, together with *singular,* trigger a forward-chaining rule that sets the goal *!singular-pronoun* for the Deictic. From *!singular-pronoun* and *!singular* (set as a goal by *singular)* the feature *"that"* is inferred, which sets the last lexical item in this clause to "that." Thus the conditional clause "you mustn't do that" has been generated. The final structure is shown in Figure 4.12.

		you	*mustn't*	*do*	*that*
		Subject	Finite	Lexverb	Residual
	mood		Modal		
		Mood		Residual	
	transitivity	Actor		Process	Goal
CLAUSE					
	ergativity	Agent		Process	Medium
		Topical			
	theme				
		Theme			
					Deictic
GROUP					
					Head
WORD			!Aux	!Verb	!Noun

Figure 4.12.

Next, the threat clause must be generated. The semantic feature $non-logical-cond sets the goal *textual-theme*, which means that the Theme of this clause will consist of both a Textual and a Topical. The feature $repeat-straight sets the goal *thesis-repetitive* (conjunction), which has the effect of lexifying the function Time as "next time". Backward-chaining from there results in Time being conflated with Conjunct, which is then conflated with Textual (an effect of *textual-theme* (clause)). Since the Textual element is ordered first (another effect

69

of *textual-theme*), "next time" can be output.

The feature *unmarked-declarative-theme,* set as a goal by *$punishment,* again conflates the Subject with the Topical, the next item to be generated. The semantic feature *$mother-punishes* sets the goal *speaker-subject* (clause), which has the effect (Subject = I), lexifying the Subject. "I" can now be output (see Figure 4.13).

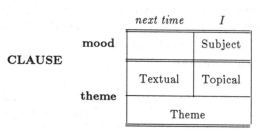

Figure 4.13.

The features *future* and *unmarked-positive* (both clause) are set as goals by *$punishment.* The feature *future* sets the goal *!will* (verb) for the Finite. The features *declarative* and *indicative* are inferred by backward-chaining from *unmarked-declarative-theme.* The feature *interactant-subject* is inferred by backward-chaining from *speaker-subject.* From *declarative, unmarked-positive,* and *interactant-subject,* the feature *reduced-posfinite* is inferred by forward-chaining, which sets the goal *!reduced* (verb) for the Finite. The feature *positive* (clause) is inferred from *unmarked-positive,* and this, together with *indicative,* allows the problem solver to infer *positive-finite,* which sets the goal *!positive* (verb) for the Finite. The forward-chaining rule shown in Figure 4.14 then fires, realizing the Finite as "'ll".

$$
\left.
\begin{array}{l}
\dots\text{!will}\underline{\qquad}\\[4pt]
\dots\text{!positive}\underline{\quad}\\[4pt]
\dots\text{!reduced}\underline{\quad}
\end{array}
\right\}
\;\underline{\;\;}\overset{\text{``ll''}}{\underset{\text{!Aux = 'll}}{}}
$$

Figure 4.14.

Since *declarative* orders the Finite just after the Subject, the Finite can be output.

The semantic feature *$smack* sets the goal *!smack* for the Process, the next item to be generated. Just like in the last clause, the feature *modalstemlexverb* is chosen, setting the goal *!stem* (verb) for the Lexverb, which is again conflated with the Process. The result is that the Process is realized as "smack".

Finally, the semantic feature $adult-centred-punishment has preselected the nominal-group features *non-possessive-nom, personal,* and *singular* for the Goal of the $Threat, and the word-rank features *!second* and *!objective* for the Head of the Goal of the $Threat ($Threat<Goal<Head). The nominal-group feature *personal* implies the feature *pronoun*, which together with *singular* triggers a forward-chaining rule that has the effect of setting the goal *!singular-pronoun* for the Head. The forward-chaining rule shown in Figure 4.15 then fires, realizing the Head (the only part of the Goal) as "you".

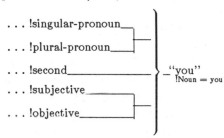

Figure 4.15.

The structure of the second clause is shown in Figure 4.16.

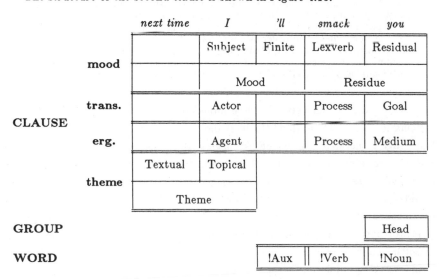

Figure 4.16.

Thus the text "you mustn't do that[,] next time I'll smack you" is generated.

4.4. Metatheoretical aspects of the conflation

Two metatheoretical aspects of the conflation should be observed at this point. Both of these involve the theory of systemic grammar being interpreted computationally—an interpretation that certainly was not intended during the development of the theory. The first point concerns the metatheoretical status of the system networks. The second point concerns the ability of the conflation to transcend certain limitations that have been associated with the computational paradigm in linguistics.

4.4.1. The status of system networks

The previous sections in this chapter have described how system networks can be interpreted as problem-solving knowledge and used to generate text. It must be stressed that from the point of view of systemic theory, this interpretation of system networks is anomalous. Halliday is careful to state that the system networks merely describe the "potential" of language, and careful not to state or imply that the system networks themselves play any role whatsoever in the "actualization" of that potential:

> [W]hen we examine the meaning potential of language itself, we find that the vast numbers of options embodied in it combine into a very few relatively independent 'networks'; and these networks of options correspond to certain basic functions of language. This enables us to give an account of the different functions of language that is relevant to the general understanding of linguistic structure rather than to any particular psychological or sociological investigation. (Halliday in deJoia and Stenton, 1980, §541)

In other words, system networks were intended to be a useful representation for systematic classification (like the periodic table in chemistry) not the actual knowledge structures from which language is generated. Yet system networks in SLANG *are* directly involved in the actualization of the meaning potential—they are exploited as problem-solving knowledge. While this is not a contradiction of Halliday's position (since no psychological claims have been put forward), it is nevertheless a different interpretation than is normally given to system networks. It is worth reiterating that the term "knowledge" here is used only in the AI sense; no claims are being made about the structure of human knowledge (see Halliday, 1978, pp. 38, 51).

4.4.2. Limitations of the computational paradigm

An interesting metatheoretical observation that can be made concerning the conflation is that the functional nature of systemic grammar may alleviate some of the important limitations of the computational paradigm. Winograd (1983, pp. 28-9) identifies three aspects of language that are ignored by the computational paradigm because they are "outside the domain of an approach that focuses on the knowledge of an individual at a particular moment." Two of the three problem areas are: the social aspects of language, and the historical aspects of language.

Turning first to the social aspects, Winograd (ibid.) says that:

> The cognitive processing approach has little to offer when, for example, we want to understand why a particular dialect is adopted by some members of society but not others, or how dialect differences play a role in establishing and maintaining group identity and cohesiveness. At the individual level, we may want to understand how linguistic devices serve to establish personal power relationships or to reinforce social distinctions of rank and status.

But these social aspects of language are a central concern of Halliday, and his functional framework was developed, to a large degree, in an attempt to address exactly these issues. Consider, for instance, one of the social phenomena mentioned by Winograd—dialect. Halliday (1978, pp. 164-82) devotes an entire chapter to one extreme form of dialect variation: antilanguages (An antilanguage is a dialect purposely developed by a group—criminals, students, etc.—intending to distance itself from mainstream society for one reason or another). He says that "the significance for the social semiotic, of the kind of variation *in the linguistic system* that we call social dialect, becomes very much clearer when we take into account the nature and functions of antilanguages" (ibid., p. 179).

> [In] the Calcutta underworld language we find not just one word for 'bomb' but twenty-one; forty-one words for 'police', and so on.... A few of these are also technical expressions for specific subcategories; but most of them are not—they are by ordinary standards synonymous, and their proliferation would be explained by students of slang as the result of a never-ending search for originality, either for the sake of liveliness and humour or, in some cases, for the sake of secrecy. (ibid., p. 165)

Dialect, and other social phenomena (including "how linguistic devices serve to establish personal power relationships or to reinforce social distinctions of rank and status" mentioned by Winograd), can be related through the description of tenor (see §3.5.2), through the interpersonal metafunction (see §3.3.8, §3.5.4) to the grammar, and through the conflation to language processing.

Turning next to the historical aspects of language, Winograd observes that

> ... some of the earlier paradigms for language study emphasized the historical side of language—the ways that languages evolve, divide, and merge. (Winograd, 1983, p. 29)

The antilanguages mentioned above are an example of languages dividing, and even the harshest critics of the functional approach admit that a functional approach is germane to the study of linguistic evolution:

> It is difficult to say what "the purpose" of language is, except, perhaps, the expression of thought, a rather empty formulation. The functions of language are various. It is unclear what might be meant by the statement that some of them are "central" or "essential".
>
> A more productive suggestion is that functional considerations determine the character of linguistic rules. Suppose it can be shown, for example, the [*sic*] some rule of English grammar facilitates a perceptual strategy for sentence analysis. Then we have the basis for a functional explanation for the linguistic rule. But several questions arise, quite apart from the matter of the source of the perceptual strategy. Is the linguistic rule a true universal? If so then the functional analysis is relevant only on the evolutionary level; human languages *must* have this rule or one like it. Suppose, on the contrary, that the linguistic rule is learned. We may still maintain the functional explanation, but it will now have to do with the evolution of English. That is, English developed in such a way as to accord with this principle. In either case, the functional explanation applies on the evolutionary level—either the evolution of the organism or of the language. (Chomsky, 1980, pp. 230-1)

Thus, the conflation of the functional theory of systemic grammar and AI problem-solving knowledge, means that the historical aspects need not be ignored in order to view "language as *a communicative process based on knowledge*" (Winograd, 1983, p. 13).

This section has discussed the metatheory of the unusual interpretation of system networks as problem-solving knowledge, and shown how this conflation brings the social and historical aspects of language within the scope of the computational paradigm.

4.5. Advantages

This chapter began by pointing out the fundamental relationship between AI problem solving and systemic grammar. It was shown that the linguistic interpretations of the concepts found in systemic linguistics can be conflated with problem-solving interpretations. The system networks found in the linguistic literature can be interpreted as sets of forward- and backward-chaining production rules forming a linguistic knowledge base; the semantic stratum as described in the systemic theory can be interpreted as compiled knowledge—rules capable of high-level inferential macromoves; the process of generating text from systemic grammars (given the interpretation just mentioned) can be interpreted as a straightforward application of general purpose AI problem-solving techniques and domain-specific knowledge to solve problems in that domain; the notion of behavioural potential can be interpreted as being described by the sum total of a problem solver's knowledge—linguistic + non-linguistic.

The fact that these two (until recently) independent fields can be conflated in this way is of theoretical and historical interest. There is, however, also an important practical significance, in that the conflation allows text generation from linguistically formalized grammars to exploit state-of-the-art AI problem-solving techniques. To date, text-generation systems have had to either pay a computational price for the use of an established linguistic formalism, or else pay a linguistic price for access to the best computational techniques (see Chapter 7). Since representations in systemic grammar and AI problem solving can be conflated, no sacrifices, linguistic or computational, need be made.

What makes text generation a hard problem (or an AI problem) is that there is a huge space of alternatives that must be discharged quickly. The discipline of AI problem solving has developed representations (e.g. production rules) for knowledge of the alternatives, and selective, efficient techniques for searching through the space of alternatives given suitably represented knowledge. The conflation of systemic grammar with problem-solving knowledge means that these sophisticated computational techniques can be exploited while the grammar (including the semantics) retains its linguistic status.

It is not surprising that systemic grammars can be processed computationally to generate text—what is significant is that unadulterated systemic grammars, as they appear in the linguistic literature, can be processed directly by the state-of-the-art knowledge-based problem-solving methods.

It is also not surprising that AI problem-solving techniques can be used to process a linguistic formalism—what is significant in this case is that given enough knowledge at the semantic stratum—note that this is within the linguistic framework—the search is optimal in the sense that it is deterministic; only steps that lead directly to a solution are taken. Thus best-case performance is achieved for the most efficient computational techniques available.

The fundamental relationship between AI problem solving and systemic grammar will ensure that SLANG retains these advantages. As better computational techniques become available, they will still be techniques for constructing a solution "selectively and efficiently from a space of alternatives." And as better systemic grammars are developed, they will still represent language as "sets of options or alternatives." As progress is made independently in each of these two fields, the SLANG approach will thus remain applicable, and will result in progressively better text-generation systems.

5
The formal model

Despite the fact the systemic grammar has a relatively long history, and has been adopted in several computer implementations (Davey, 1978; Mann and Matthiessen, 1983), it has never been rigorously formalized in the way that traditional grammars have. The reason for this appears to be that the formal tools applied to traditional structural (syntagmatic) grammars are not so easily applied to a functional theory. In addition, it seems that the "rigorous rules" used to formalize traditional grammars are viewed by systemic linguists as inherently structural (e.g. Halliday, 1978, pp. 191-2). The formal model of systemic grammar presented here will involve "rigorous rules" but will not compromise the functional perspective. This formalization will allow the definition of such notions as the language generated by a grammar, and the demonstration of results relating to properties of a generation algorithm based on the previous chapter. The central issues discussed include the correctness and efficiency of this algorithm.

Two warnings should be given concerning this formal model. First, the generation algorithm presented (§5.3 and §5.4) is based on the description of systemic grammar presented in Chapter 3 which was in turn based partly on Halliday (1978). As a result of certain assumptions (especially concerning the input to the generation—in this case involving preselection), it may not be compatible with models based on other versions of the theory. Second, this formalization is largely exploratory, in that it is meant to investigate and illustrate the possibility of providing a rigorous formalization of systemic grammar suitable for defining a generation mechanism—it is not meant to be the definitive formalization of systemic grammar.

The first section of the formal model will describe the syntactic structures specified by systemic grammars. This will require a more complex treatment than for many other grammars because of the need to interrelate constituency and the sophisticated functional treatment of structure. The next section (§5.2) defines a systemic grammar and gives a declarative definition of the language generated by the grammar. The grammar is defined using familiar terms such as "feature," "system," "grammatical function" and "terminal symbol"; but the notion of a system network will be defined in terms of a set of production rules which embody the same information.

The first two sections deal only with abstract systemic ideas and should be applicable to any systemic model. In contrast, §5.3 describes a specific generation algorithm based on Chapter 4, involving forward- and backward-chaining of production rules. The fourth section proves some results about the behaviour of this generation algorithm given certain kinds of inputs.

Regardless of the method used to search the system network, the systemic syntactic structures will be specified by realization rules attached to the features found during that search. The fifth section presents a typical set of realization relationships (those described in Chapter 3) and an algorithm for constructing structures from these is outlined in §5.6. Realization rules in systemic grammar can be interpreted both as a declaration of some characteristics a structure must have, and as a procedure for modifying partial descriptions of a structure during generation. Both of these interpretations are usefully captured in §5.7 where realization rules are formulated as rules in logic. The generation algorithm is expressed as "problem reduction" in §5.8.

5.1. Systemic syntactic structures

Before defining a systemic grammar, the structures characterized by systemic grammars will be defined. (As in many formal definitions, there is a problem concerning the order of presentation, as many definitions are mutually dependent.) One traditional notion that is needed is that of a "tree":

> A *tree* is a finite set of *nodes* connected by directed *edges*, which satisfy the following three conditions (if an edge is directed from node 1 to node

2, we say the edge *leaves* node 1 and *enters* node 2):

1) There is exactly one node which no edge enters. This node is called the *root*.

2) For each node in the tree there exists a sequence of directed edges from the root to the node. Thus the tree is connected.

3) Exactly one edge enters every node except the root. As a consequence there are no loops in the tree. (Hopcroft and Ullman, 1969, pp. 18-20.)

An important relationship between nodes in a tree is "descendancy":

> The set of all nodes n, such that there is an edge leaving a given node m and entering n, is called the *direct descendants* of m. A node n is called a descendant of node m if there is a sequence of nodes $n_1, n_2, \ldots, n_k$ such that $n_k = n$, $n_1 = m$, and for each i, n_{i+1} is a direct descendant of n_i. We shall, by convention, say a node is a direct descendant of itself. (ibid.)

A *leaf node* or *terminal node* of a tree is a node that has no descendants. A tree will be represented by a pair (A, p) where A is a finite set—the "nodes" of the tree—and p is the partial function from A to A which maps every node (except the root node) to its parent node. Further, an ordering must be imposed on certain trees, to reflect the idea of left-right order in syntactic structure. An *ordered tree* is one in which a binary, irreflexive asymmetric transitive relation is defined upon nodes such that:

if $n_1 < n_2$, m_1 a descendant of n_1, m_2 a descendant of n_2, then $m_1 < m_2$;

if m_1 is a descendant of n_1 then neither $n_1 < m_1$ nor $m_1 < n_1$;

if m_1 and m_2 are direct descendants of n_1, with $n_1 \neq m_1$, $n_1 \neq m_2$, $m_1 \neq m_2$, then either $m_1 < m_2$ or $m_2 < m_1$.

An ordered tree will be written as a triple $(N, p, <)$ where N is the set of nodes, p is the parent function, (see above), and $<$ is the "left-right" ordering relation.

Within systemic grammar, each constituent has one or more "functional analyses," each of which is a simultaneous hierarchical decomposition of the constituent. Such a decomposition can be represented as a labelled tree, where each node apart from the root is labelled with some grammatical function.

Defn. 1.1:

Let V be some finite set. A *functional analysis over V* is a pair $((A, p), h)$ where (A, p) is a tree and h is an injective mapping from the non-root nodes of (A, p) to V.

Defn. 1.2:

Let $V_1, \ldots V_m$ be a family of finite sets. A *constituent analysed with respect to* $V_1, \ldots V_m$ consists of a triple $c = ((A_1, \ldots A_m), B, g)$ where:

(a) each A_i is a functional analysis over V_i.

(b) B is a finite set (the *daughter nodes* of c).

(c) g is a mapping from B to the powerset of the set of terminal nodes in the trees in $A_1, \ldots A_m$ (i.e. for every daughter node n, $g(n)$ is a set of leaf nodes from the trees in the m functional analyses $A_1, \ldots A_m$).

The above definition allows the structural parts of a constituent (which will be a set of daughter nodes) to be linked to the various functional analyses of that constituent. Each daughter node is linked to one or more of the leaves of the functional analyses.

Defn. 1.3:

A *grammatical function scheme* is an ordered sequence $(R_1, \ldots R_k)$ of families of finite sets. (That is, each R_i is of the form $\{V_1, \ldots V_m\}$ (for some m), each V_j being a finite set.) In such a scheme, R_i is said to be "at rank i."

Informally, R_i represents the set of functions available at rank i, which are grouped into sets to reflect the fact that, at a given rank, the grammatical functions are grouped according to availability for functional analyses of a constituent at that rank. Lower rank numbers correspond, loosely speaking, to larger constituent sizes—*clause* has a lower rank number than *group*, etc.

It is now necessary to define the nature of a syntactic structure within the model. Informally, this consists of a conventional ordered tree (i.e. a set of constituents, hierarchically connected), where each constituent has one or more functional analyses, in the sense of definitions 1.1 and 1.2 above, and where the leaf nodes of the tree are associated with terminal symbols.

Defn. 1.4:

Let $S = (R_1, \ldots R_k)$ be a grammatical function scheme, and Vt some finite set. A *systemic syntactic structure within S and Vt* consists of a tuple $T = (C, r, M, <, L)$ such that:

(a) C is a finite set $\{c_1, \ldots c_t\}$, where each c_i is a constituent analysed with respect to some R_j in S. (The set consisting of all the nodes of the various trees in the functional analyses of the constituents in C is called the set of *function nodes* of the structure T.)

(b) r is an item (the *root node*) distinct from all daughter nodes in constituents in C.

(c) Let N denote the set of all daughter nodes in constituents in C. M is a total function from N to $N \cup \{r\}$ and $<$ is an ordering relation on N such that:

(i) $(N \cup \{r\}, M, <)$ is an ordered tree,

(ii) within each constituent $c \in C$, $M(n)$ is the same for each daughter node n in c_j,

(iii) there is exactly one constituent c_j such that $M(n) = r$ for each daughter node n in c_j,

(iv) if $M(n_1) = n_2$ then n_1 and n_2 are in distinct constituents in C.

(d) L is a mapping from the leaf nodes of the tree $(N \cup \{r\}, M, <)$ to Vt.

In a structure as above, $N \cup \{r\}$ is called the set of *unit nodes* of the structure, and $(N \cup \{r\}, M, <)$ is called the *constituent tree* of the structure.

Defn. 1.5:

In a systemic syntactic structure as above, if c is a constituent in C analysed with respect to R_j (where $1 \leq j \leq k$), then c is said to be *at rank* j, and if $M(n_1) = n_2$, n_1 is in a constituent c_1 at rank j_1, n_2 is in a constituent c_2 at rank j_2, and $j_2 \geq j_1$, then c_1 is said to be *rankshifted* (see §3.3.6).

Defn. 1.6:

Let $S = (R_1, \ldots R_k)$ be a grammatical function scheme, and Vt some finite set. Let $T = (C, r, M, <, L)$ be a systemic syntactic structure within S and Vt. Then the *terminal string of* T is the sequence s of elements of Vt defined by a traversal of the leaves of the tree $(N \cup \{r\}, M, <)$ in ascending ("left-right") order. That is, $s = (L(n_1), \ldots L(n_t))$ where $\{n_1, \ldots n_t\}$ is the set of leaf nodes of $(N \cup \{r\}, M, <)$ and where $n_i < n_{i+1}$ for every i from 1 to $t-1$.

5.2. A formalization of systemic grammar

First, some basic definitions are needed for some constructs which are used in the definition of a systemic grammar. Each constituent has to be associated with a feature-set from the systemic grammar, which will contribute to characterizing its grammatical well-formedness.

Defn. 2.1:

Let $S=(R_1,...R_k)$ be a grammatical function scheme, and Vt some finite set. Let $T=(C,r,M,<,L)$ be a systemic syntactic structure within S and Vt. Let $F=(F_1,...F_k)$ be a family of disjoint finite sets. A *feature-assignment from T to F* is a mapping h from C to the powerset of $F_1\cup F_2,...\cup F_k$ such that for any node $c\in C$ at rank j $(1\leq j\leq k)$, $h(c)$ is a subset of some F_j (i.e. for any constituent c in C, $h(c)$ is a subset of exactly one of the sets in F).

Defn. 2.2:

Suppose S is a grammatical function scheme, F is a family of disjoint finite sets and Vt is a finite set. Let $SS(S,Vt)$ denote the set of systemic syntactic structures within S and Vt. Let $FA(S,Vt,F)$ denote the set of feature-assignments from $SS(S,Vt)$ to F. Let $CON(T)$ be the set of constituents in a systemic syntactic structure T (where T is in $SS(S,Vt)$). A *realization rule based on S, F and Vt* is a mapping from triples of the form (T,h,c) (where $T\in SS(S,Vt)$, $h\in FA(S,Vt,F)$ and $c\in CON(T)$) to the set $\{0,1\}$.

That is, a realization rule is a mapping which given a syntactic structure, a feature labelling, and a particular constituent in the structure, yields either 0 or 1 (intuitively "false" or "true" respectively). These rules can be viewed as predicates over feature-labelled syntactic structures, in which one constituent is taken as a point of reference. A triple (T,h,c) where T is a syntactic structure, h is a feature-assignment, and c is a constituent in C, is said to *satisfy* a realization rule J if $J(T,h,c)=1$, and is said to satisfy a set of realization rules if it satisfies each rule in the set.

System networks will be defined below as rules which stipulate permissible combinations of features, using conjunction and disjunction (both ordinary and exclusive) to combine them. Thus various basic definitions concerning feature sets are required.

Defn. 2.3:

Let A be some finite set such that $\emptyset$ (the empty set) is not an element of A. A *logical expression over A* is either:

(a) an element of A,

(b) a tuple $(0, a_1, a_2, \ldots a_n)$ where the a_i are logical expressions over A. (Conventionally, such a triple will be written "$a_1 \vee a_2 \ldots \vee a_n$," or "$a_1$ OR $a_2 \ldots$ OR a_n," and will be called a "disjunctive logical expression."),

(c) a tuple $(1, a_1, a_2, \ldots a_n)$ where the a_i are logical expressions over A. (Conventionally, such a triple will be written "$a_1 \wedge a_2 \ldots \wedge a_n$," or "$a_1$ AND $a_2 \ldots$ AND a_n," and will be called a "conjunctive logical expression.")

Defn. 2.4:

Let Q be a logical expression over some set A, and B be some subset of A. Then B is said to *satisfy* Q if either:

(a) $Q = a$ for some element a of B

(b) $Q = (0, Q_1, \ldots Q_n)$ and B satisfies at least one of $Q_1, \ldots Q_n$

(c) $Q = (1, Q_1, \ldots Q_n)$ and B satisfies all of $Q_1, \ldots Q_n$.

Defn. 2.5:

Let Q be a logical expression over some set A, and c be some element of A. Then c is *mentioned in* Q if either:

(a) $c = Q$

(b) $Q = (N, a_1, \ldots a_n)$ (for some N in $\{0, 1\}$) and c is mentioned in at least one of $a_1, \ldots a_n$.

Defn. 2.6:

Let $Q = (N, a_1, \ldots a_n)$ (for some N in $\{0, 1\}$) be a logical expression over some set A, and c be some element of A. Then c is *a term in* Q if $c = a_i$, for some i.

Defn. 2.7:

Let Q be a logical expression over some set A, and c be some element of A. Then c *occurs purely conjunctively in* Q if either:

(a) $c = Q$,

(b) $Q = (1, a_1, \ldots a_n)$ and c occurs purely conjunctively in some a_i.

Notice that if a set B satisfies a logical expression Q, and c occurs purely conjunctively in Q, then it must be the case that $c \in B$. Also, since there is no logical negation in these definitions, if all the features mentioned in an expression Q are in a set B, then B must satisfy Q.

Defn. 2.8:

> Let A be a finite set. Then a *production over A* is a pair (Q, b) where Q
> is either the empty set (written "$\emptyset$") or a logical expression over A, and
> b is an element of A.

Now a definition of a systemic grammar can be presented. A system network will
be defined as a set of productions, in the above sense, which impose constraints
on feature-combinations, and each of which has a set of structural constraints
associated with it ("realization rules" in the sense of Defn. 2.2 above).

Defn. 2.9:

> A *systemic grammar* is a pair $(VT, NETWORKS)$ where $NETWORKS$ is a
> finite sequence $(N_1, ... N_k)$ such that each N_i is a tuple (F_i, Ψ_i, VN_i, P_i)
> where:
>
> (a) F_i is a finite set (the *features*), such that F_i and F_j are disjoint if
> $i \neq j$;
>
> (b) Ψ_i is a set of proper subsets of the set F_i (the *systems*);
>
> (c) VN_i is a finite set $\{A_1, ... A_m\}$ of finite sets—the elements of each A_i
> are *functions* which act as grammatical labels within the functional ana-
> lyses of a constituent;
>
> (d) P_i is a finite set of pairs (p, R) where p is a production (ξ, α) over
> F_i, and R is a set of realization rules based on $(VN_1, ... VN_k)$, $(F_1, ... F_k)$ and
> VT. (These will normally be written "$\xi \to \alpha, R$", and any rule r in R will
> be said to be "associated with" α.) Each feature α in F_i appears exactly
> once in a production of the form $\xi \to \alpha, R$, and for any system S in Ψ,
> there is a single ξ such that every feature α in S appears in a production
> of the form $\xi \to \alpha, R$ for some R (i.e. all the features in a system have the
> same entry conditions).
>
> VT is a finite set (the *terminal symbols*), disjoint from all the sets F_i and
> from all the sets in the VN_i.

It is often convenient to consider the separate portions of a systemic grammar
individually, so a tuple $(F_i, \Psi_i, VN_i, VT, P_i)$ (for some i) will be called a *system network*.

Defn. 2.10:

Suppose (F, Ψ, VN, VT, P) is a system network as above. A subset ω of F is said to be *consistent* if there are no features $\alpha, \beta \in \omega$ and system $\Sigma \in \Psi$ such that $\alpha \in \Sigma \ \& \ \beta \in \Sigma \ \& \ \alpha \neq \beta$.

Defn. 2.11:

Suppose (F, Ψ, VN, VT, P) is a system network as above. A subset ω of F is said to be *valid* if it is a consistent feature set such that:

(a) There is no production $\xi \to \alpha, R$ in P such that ξ is satisfied by ω but there is no β in ω such that $\xi \to \beta, R'$ is in P (i.e. if an entry condition is satisfied, there must be at least one feature with that entry condition present in ω).

(b) There are no productions $\xi \to \alpha, R$ such that $\alpha \in \omega$, but ξ is not satisfied by ω.

Defn. 2.12:

Suppose (F, Ψ, VN, VT, P) is a system network as above. A subset ω of F is said to be *conflicting* if there is no valid subset ϕ of F such that $\omega \subseteq \phi$. (Similarly, a subset ω is said to be *non-conflicting* if there exists a valid subset of F which is a superset of ω.)

The distinction between "consistent" and "non-conflicting" (or between "inconsistent" and "conflicting") may not be obvious at once. An analogy with sets of logical formulae may be useful in clarifying this point. "Inconsistency" here is similar to the explicit presence of a contradiction in a set of formulae (P and $\neg P$), whereas "conflicting" is comparable to a contradiction being derivable from the set of formulae. "Consistent" is local to a system, and can be checked directly; "non-conflicting" is more global and can be checked only by a computation equivalent to carrying out a complete derivation. Notice that a non-conflicting set is necessarily consistent—this follows from the definition of "valid."

Often, when discussing a systemic grammar, it is convenient to allude to all the features, functions, and terminal symbols in the grammar, without distinguishing different networks. Therefore, given a grammar $G = (VT, (N_1, ... N_k))$, where each $N_i = (F_i, \Psi_i, VN_i, P_i)$, the notation may refer to G as a quintuple $[F, \Psi, Vn, Vt, P]$ where $F = (F_1, ... F_k)$, $\Psi = \Psi_1 \cup \Psi_2 ... \cup \Psi_k$ and $VN = (VN_1, ... VN_k)$. That is, F is an ordered family of feature-sets, Vn is a grammatical function scheme in the sense of Defn. 1.3, and Vt is simply the complete set of terminal symbols.

For further convenience, a feature α may be referred to as being "in F," when what is meant is that α is an element of some F_i.

The grammar has been presented but the language it generates has not yet been defined. First a definition must be given for how a syntactic structure is characterized by the grammar. The essential idea is that a pair consisting of a systemic structure and a feature-assignment is well-formed if each constituent is assigned a valid feature set, and all the realization rules which are linked to constituents by the feature-assignment and the grammar are satisfied by the structure.

Defn. 2.13:

Let G be a systemic grammar $[F, \Psi, Vn, Vt, P]$. Let $T = (C, r, M, <, L)$ be a systemic syntactic structure within Vn and Vt. Let h be a feature-assignment from T to F. Then (T, h) is said to be *well-formed with respect to G* if, for every constituent $c \in C$:

(a) $h(C)$ is a valid feature set,

(b) (T, h, c) satisfies every realization rule associated with (see Defn. 2.9(d)) every feature in $h(c)$.

Defn. 2.14:

Let G be a systemic grammar as in the above definition. A string s of elements of Vt is said to be *generated* by G if there exists a systemic syntactic structure T within Vn and Vt, and a feature-assignment h from T to F, such that (T, h) is well-formed with respect to G and s is the terminal string of the constituent tree of T.

The set of strings generated by a grammar G is called "the language generated by G" and is written "$L(G)$".

5.3. Generation

The definition of $L(G)$ above was independent of any notion of generating a syntactic structure from some initial set of features—it simply stated what constituted a well-formed structure (and hence string). To relate these notions to some notion of generation or computation, it is useful to consider the notion of a process which starts from some initial specification (e.g. some partial structure) and computes a well-formed structure according to that description. Patten (1986) defines a method for doing exactly this, by operating on a *feature heap* which is, roughly, a set of syntactic constituents labelled with clusters of features. The generation process consists of expanding the labelling of each constituent until it is a valid feature set (in the sense defined in §5.2 above), with each selected feature's realization rules being used to build up a fuller picture of what the eventual structure will be. The partial structure maintained during this process consists of the feature heap (i.e. the labelled constituents so far constructed) and a record of all the stipulations imposed by the realization rules—adjacency, expansion, conflation, lexification, etc. Section 5.6 below outlines a formalization of the structure-building process, but first the concentration will be placed on another aspect of the generation mechanism, namely the generation of valid feature sets from initial feature sets. This is a computation which proceeds locally, within a system network, and so a simplification has been introduced where other aspects of the generation are ignored, and the emphasis is placed in the issue of using the information in a single system network to generate a valid set of features. Informally, this should be acceptable since entry condition features apply to the same unit as the features for which they are entry conditions (e.g. if *indicative* is generated from *declarative*, these two features should both refer to a particular clause). In fact the constituent remains constant during a generation within any particular system network. (Any features in the clause network that are generated—however indirectly—from *declarative* will still refer to the same clause as *declarative*.)

Defn. 3.1:

Given a systemic grammar $G=[F,\Psi,Vn,Vt,P]$, where $F=(F_1,...F_k)$, a *generation relationship* is a binary relation "$\Rightarrow$" between subsets of the sets F_i, such that

(a) if $A\Rightarrow B$ then there is exactly one F_i such that $A\subseteq F_i$, and $B\subseteq F_i$.

(b) if $A\Rightarrow B$ then $A\subseteq B$.

Suppose that $\omega_1, \omega_2, \omega_3,...\omega_m$ are feature sets such that $\omega_1\rightarrow\omega_2, \omega_2\rightarrow\omega_3, ..., \omega_{m-1}\Rightarrow\omega_m$. Then it is said that $\omega_1\Rightarrow^*\omega_m$, and that ω_1 *generates* ω_m. By convention $\omega\Rightarrow^*\omega$.

Alternative generation processes will embody different generation relationships—the following definitions correspond to the generator described in Chapter 4.

Defn. 3.2:

(a) In a system network (F,Ψ,VN,VT,P) as defined above, an *S-feature* is a feature α such that either $\alpha\in\bigcup(\Psi)$ ($\bigcup(\Psi)$ denotes the union of the sets in Ψ. For example, if Ψ is a set of sets $\{A,B,C,...M\}$ then

$\bigcup(\Psi) = A \cup B \cup C ... \cup M.$) or there is a production $\xi \to \beta, R$ in P where β is an S-feature and α is mentioned in ξ. (Informally, α is in a system or is an entry conditions for an S-feature.)

(b) Any member of F that is not an S-feature is defined to be a *G-feature*.

Defn. 3.3:

A production $\xi \to \beta, R$ is said to be a *gate* if β is a G-feature.

Informally, the initial feature set for the generation consists of those features preselected by higher ranks or by the semantic stratum. These initial features acts as goals or constraints that guide the search through the grammar—the generation is that search. The initial features will typically be scattered through the middle of the system network, and the generation proceeds from these in two opposite directions—toward the left of the network through progressively less delicate systems (generating S-features), and toward the right through the gates (generating G-features).

Defn. 3.4:

Suppose ω is a feature set from a system network $N = (F, \Psi, VN, VT, P)$. If $\xi \to \delta, R$ is a production in P, then

(a) $\omega \Rightarrow \omega \cup \{\delta\}$ when ω satisfies ξ and δ is a G-feature.

(b) $\omega \Rightarrow \omega \cup \{\alpha\}$ when

    (i) α occurs purely conjunctively in ξ

    (ii) $\delta \in \omega$

    (iii) δ is an S-feature

    (iv) there is no system $S \in \Psi$ such that $\alpha \in S$ and there is a $\beta \in S$, $\beta \neq \alpha$, $\beta \in \omega$.

In each case the production $\xi \to \delta, R$ is *applied* to feature set ω. (a) and (b) are *forward-* and *backward-applications* respectively. Thus "$\Rightarrow$" relates two feature sets exactly when the second is obtained from the first by the application of a single production, and for two feature sets ϕ and ω, $\omega \Rightarrow^* \phi$ if ϕ can be obtained from ω by application of some number of productions of P. If all the steps are forward-applications, say ω generates ϕ by "forward-chaining"—*mutatis mutandis*, ω may also generate ϕ by "backward-chaining," or by a combination of the two.

5.4. Soundness and completeness

To show that a generation relationship is an appropriate generation mechanism, it must be demonstrated that it generates only valid feature sets, and that any valid feature set can be generated in this way. This is analogous to proving the correctness of an inference mechanism in formal logic—the first condition is analogous to soundness, and the second to completeness. It might be thought that "soundness" would be defined in terms of preserving validity of feature sets. In fact, since many generation processes (including the one defined in §5.3 above) will be driven by invalidity (features added to the feature set to try to achieve a valid feature set), it will not be the case that "$\Rightarrow$" preserves validity at all stages. What matters is the validity of the final feature set produced by "$\Rightarrow$"; i.e. the set of features when no further productions can be applied.

It is not very useful to discuss soundness of a generation relationship in isolation from assumptions about initial feature sets, since generation relations tend to be devised to work appropriately with particular kinds of initial feature sets. The appropriate soundness result for the relationship defined in Defn. 3.4 above is the following:

Soundness theorem: If ω_0 is a non-conflicting feature set, and $\omega_0 \Rightarrow \omega'$, then ω' is non-conflicting.

Proof: Since ω_0 is non-conflicting, there is some superset ϕ of ω_0 which is valid.

(a) Suppose $\omega_0 \Rightarrow \omega_0 \cup \{\alpha\}$ by Defn. 3.4(a); that is, using a production $\xi \to \alpha, R$ where α is a G-feature. Since ω_0 satisfies ξ, ϕ must contain α (by Defn. 2.11(a) for "valid"). Hence ϕ is a valid superset of $\omega_0 \cup \{\alpha\}$. Hence $\omega_0 \cup \{\alpha\}$ is non-conflicting.

(b) Suppose $\omega_0 \Rightarrow \omega_0 \cup \{\alpha\}$ by Defn. 3.4(b); that is, using a production $\xi \to \delta, R$ where δ is an S-feature and α occurs purely conjunctively in ξ. Since ω_0 contains δ, ψ must satisfy ξ (by Defn. 2.11(b) for "valid") Hence, since α occurs purely conjunctively in ξ, it must be that case that $\alpha \in \phi$ (see remark following Defn. 2.7). Hence ϕ is a valid superset of $\omega_0 \cup \{\alpha\}$, which is therefore a non-conflicting feature set.

Corollary: If ω_0 is a non-conflicting feature set, and $\omega_0 \Rightarrow^* \omega'$, then ω' is non-conflicting.

It is interesting to note that this proof does not make explicit use of part (b)(iv) of Defn. 3.4. An implementation of the "$\Rightarrow$" generation algorithm which omitted checks on the consistency of its feature choices would therefore still be sound *providing the original feature set was non-conflicting.*

Lemma 1: If $\omega \Rightarrow \omega \cup \{\delta\}$, and δ is not in ω, then ω is not valid.

Proof: If $\omega \Rightarrow \cup \{\delta\}$, then there are two cases:

(i)   There is a production $\xi \rightarrow \delta, R$ where δ is a G-feature and ω satisfies ξ. Since δ is not in ω, this would mean that ω is not valid (by Defn. 2.11(a)).

(ii) There is a production $\xi \rightarrow \alpha, R$ where α is an S-feature, δ occurs purely conjunctively in ξ, and $\alpha \in \omega$. Since δ is not in ω, ω does not satisfy ξ, despite containing α. This would mean that ω is not valid (by Defn. 2.11(b)).

Corollary: If ω is valid, then there is no feature set ω' such that $\omega \subset \omega'$ and $\omega \Rightarrow^* \omega'$.

These results also suggest that if there is a sequence of feature-sets $\omega_1 \Rightarrow \omega_2 \Rightarrow ...$, where ω_1 is non-conflicting, then this sequence is bound to lead to a valid feature set (since size of the feature set increases at each step, and only finite feature sets are involved).

Defining completeness is similarly complicated by the issue of initial feature sets. Clearly, since $\omega \Rightarrow^* \omega$ for any feature set ω, it will trivially be the case that any valid feature set can be generated via any reasonable generation relationship (i.e. from itself). A particular variant of "completeness" will be proven for the generation relationship given in Defn. 3.4 above, but it will not be regarded as appropriate to attempt a fully general definition of completeness.

As mentioned in §5.3 above, the generation relationship of Defn. 3.4 is devised to operate on an initial set of preselected features spread throughout the network. In order to discuss the completeness of the relationship, it is first necessary to give a precise definition of how those initial features should be distributed; the next few definitions provide that characterization.

Defn. 4.1:

For any feature set ω, a feature $\alpha \in \omega$ is a *seed feature with respect to* ω if (a) it is an S-feature and (b) there is no production $\xi \rightarrow \beta, R$ such that β is an S-feature in ω and α occurs purely conjunctively in ξ.

Informally, a seed feature is an S-feature which cannot be generated by backward-chaining (Defn. 3.4(b)) from other features in the set.

Defn. 4.2:

A feature α is *immediately less delicate than* a feature δ if and only if P contains a production $\xi \rightarrow \delta, R$ and α is mentioned in ξ.

Defn. 4.3:

A feature α is *less delicate than* a feature δ if and only if either (a) α is immediately less delicate than δ; or (b) there is a feature β such that α is less delicate than β and β is immediately less delicate than δ.

Traditionally, features at the right-hand side of a system network are more "delicate" in the sense of representing a finer classification of linguistic entities.

Defn. 4.4:

A feature α is a *root feature* if $\emptyset \rightarrow \alpha, R \in P$ (i.e. if it has no entry conditions—a least delicate feature: e.g. *clause, nominal-group*, etc.).

Defn. 4.5:

A system network is *acyclic* if the "less delicate than" relation over P is a strict partial order.

The notion of an acyclic network will be used to restrict the discussion to those grammars that do not contain recursive systems (see §3.3.9). Notice that this does not rule out recursive syntactic structures, since a recursive system affects only the feature configurations for a particular constituent.

Defn. 4.6:

An S-feature α is said to be a *most delicate S-feature* if there is no S-feature β such that α is less delicate than β.

Defn. 4.7:

A system network is *expressive* if all root features are S-features. (Informally, the system network must have at least one system.)

Completeness theorem: Let $N = (F, \Psi, VN, VT, P)$ be an acyclic expressive system network. Let ω be a valid subset of F. There exists a non-conflicting set of features ω_0 such that each element of ω_0 is a seed with respect to ω, and $\omega_0 \Rightarrow^* \omega$.

91

Proof:[4] Let ω_0 be the set of all features in ω which are seeds with respect to ω. ω_0 must be non-conflicting, since ω is valid. Let ω_1 be a feature set such that $\omega_0 \Rightarrow^* \omega_1$, and such that there is no $\omega_2 \neq \omega_1$ with $\omega_1 \Rightarrow \omega_2$ (i.e. ω_1 is a maximal set generated from ω_0). It will be shown that every feature in ω lies in ω_1. Since ω is valid, it follows by Lemma 1 that this set ω_1 must equal ω, and the result follows. The proof proceeds separately for S-features and G-features.

(a) *S-features.* Suppose $\alpha \in \omega$ is an S-feature.

> (i) If α is a seed feature with respect to ω, then it follows that $\alpha \in \omega_1$ since $\alpha \in \omega_0$, and $\omega_0 \subseteq \omega_1$.

> (ii) Suppose α is not a seed feature with respect to ω. Then α must occur purely conjunctively in the left-hand side of a production which has an S-feature β on the right-hand side, and where $\beta \in \omega$. If β is in ω_0 (i.e. is a seed with respect to ω), then β is in ω_1, so by Defn. 3.4(b) α is in ω_1 (since ω_1 is maximal). On the other hand, if β is not in ω_0 (i.e. is not a seed with respect to ω), then a similar argument can be applied to β, using the fact that there must be some rule in which β occurs purely conjunctively, with an S-feature γ that is in ω on the right-hand side. This sequence of features α, β, γ, ... must eventually terminate at a seed feature with respect to ω, since the network is acyclic and most delicate S-features are seeds with respect to any feature set which contains them. Hence, all the features in the sequence, including α, are in ω_1.

(b) *G-features.* This proof is by induction on the *depth* of a G-feature, where the "depth" of a G-feature γ is defined to be the length of the longest sequence of features $\{\alpha_1, ... \alpha_M\}$ such that α_1 is a root feature, $\alpha_M = \gamma$, and for each i, α_i is immediately less delicate than α_{i+1}. (Informally, the depth of a feature is the length of the longest path from the left side of the network to the feature.) Suppose it has been proven that the theorem holds for all G-features of depth less than or equal to N (i.e. every such G-feature lies in ω_1), where $N > 1$. Let β be a G-feature of depth $N+1$, appearing in a production $\xi \to \beta, R$. (Each feature appears on the right-hand side of exactly one production—see Defn. 2.9.) Each feature mentioned in ξ must either be an S-feature or a G-feature of depth less than $N+1$. Hence each feature mentioned in ξ is in ω_1 (assuming part (a) of the proof above). Hence ω_1 must satisfy ξ (see remark following Defn. 2.7). Therefore, by Defn. 3.4(a) and the fact that ω_1 is the maximal set generated from ω_0, β must be in ω_1.

Since the network is expressive, there are no G-features of depth 1, and G-features of depth 2 have entry conditions which are entirely made up of S-features. By part (a) of the proof, it follows that all the features mentioned in the entry conditions of G-features of depth 2 are in ω_1, and hence all depth 2 G-features are in ω_1. This establishes the induction.

5.5. Some realization rules

Realization rules, thus far, have simply been described as mappings from triples (T,h,c) to $\{0,1\}$. It is expected that some basic set of these mappings will be provided by systemic theory, to be used as needed in writing systemic grammars. That is, there will not be arbitrary mappings defined for each new gramamr, but a small repertoire of realization rules will serve for a wide range of grammars. The realization rules used by different systemic writers vary slightly, but the following are typical (taken from Chapter 3). Assume a systemic grammar $G=[F,\Psi,Vn,Vt,P]$, a systemic syntactic structure $T=(C,r,M,<,L)$, and a feature-assignment h; A and B are any grammatical functions from the sets in Vn, α is in F, a is in Vt.

Adjacency. The notation "$A \; \hat{} \; B$", where A and B are functions from the same set of functions at some rank, is taken to mean the mapping R -*adjacent* $[A,B]$ which is 1 for (T,h,c) iff there exist two daughter nodes m_1 and m_2 in c such that $m_1<m_2$, there is no m_3 with $m_1<m_3<m_2$, m_1 is associated with a node in the functional analysis which has the grammatical function A, and m_2 is similarly associated with the grammatical function B.

Expansion. The notation "$A(B)$", where A and B are functions from the same set of functions at some rank, denotes the mapping R -*expands* $[A,B]$ which is 1 for (T,h,c) iff the functional analyses of c include one in which there is a node n, which is associated with the function A and a node m, a direct descendant of n, which is associated with B.

Conflation. The notation "$A \; / \; B$" denotes the mapping R -*conflated* $[A,B]$ which is 1 for (T,h,c) iff there is a daughter node n in c such that n is associated with both grammatical functions A and B (via its links to nodes in the functional analyses).

Lexify. The notation "$A = a$" denotes the mapping R -*lexify* $[A,a]$ which is 1 if there is a terminal node m which is a daughter of c, such that $L(m)=a$, and m is associated with the grammatical function A.

Preselection. The notation "$A_1<A_2<...<A_i:\alpha$" denotes the mapping R -*preselects* $[A_1,A_2,...A_i,\alpha]$ which is 1 for (T,h,c) iff there is a descendency line of daughter nodes $(n_1,...n_i)$ such that n_1 is in c, $M(n_{j+1})=n_j$ (for $j=1$ to $i-1$), n_j is associated with A_j ($j=1$ to i), and $\alpha\in h(n_i)$.

Aside from the fact that different realization relations and notations may be used, a similar treatment of realization will appear in any systemic model.

5.6. Generating structures.

As described in §5.3 and §5.4, the design of a generation algorithm for this systemic model consists largely of devising an algorithm which, given a set of initial features for a set of constituents, produces a derivation of a valid feature set for each constituent using the productions of the grammar (equivalent to traversing the system networks, collecting features). Such an algorithm should have, as a side-effect, the development of a syntactic structure (as defined in §5.1 above) using the information in the realization rules attached to the selected features. Each realization rule makes some very local, limited statement about the final structure (in terms of adjacency, conflation etc.). The generator must accumulate these statements or constraints as contributions to the description of the final structure.

A systemic syntactic structure can be regarded as being characterized by various relationships, which embody the information required in the definitions in §5.1. Assuming a systemic grammar $G = [F, \Psi, Vn, Vt, P]$, the approach will be to build up sets of nodes, constituents, functional analyses, and feature-assignments which will eventually form a syntactic structure $T = (C, r, M, <, L)$. Various dynamically altering sets of entities are required—DN (a set of daughter nodes), C (a set of constituents), FN (a set of function nodes); and various relations defined on these sets and on the sets from the grammar—F (a set of features), Vn' (the set of grammatical functions in the scheme Vn), Vt (a set of lexical items).

The relationships needed are:

$NEXT$, subset of $DN \times DN$: (dn_1, dn_2) are in $NEXT$ iff dn_1 and dn_2 are in the same constituent and immediately adjacent according to the left-right order, $dn_1 < dn_2$.

$DAUGHTER$, subset of $DN \times C$: (dn_1, c) are in $DAUGHTER$ iff dn_1 is in the constituent c.

$MOTHER$, subset of $DN \times DN$: (dn_1, dn_2) are in $MOTHER$ if $M(dn_1) = dn_2$, where M is the mapping described in Defn. 1.4.

$HAS\text{-}FUNCTION$, subset of $DN \times FN$: (dn_1, fn_1) are in $HAS\text{-}FUNCTION$ iff fn_1 is in the set $g(dn_1)$, where g is the mapping described in Defn. 1.2 (i.e. the node dn_1 is associated with fn_1 in the functional analysis).

SAME –NODE , subset of $DN \times C$: (dn_1,c) are in *SAME –NODE* iff the daughter node dn_1 corresponds to the constituent c. I.e., if *SAME –NODE* (dn_1,c), then for all dn_k such that *DAUGHTER* (dn_k,c), it is implied that *MOTHER* (dn_k,dn_1). This is for notational convenience only.

HAS –FEATURE , subset of $C \times F$: (c,y) are in *HAS –FEATURE* iff y is in the set $f(C)$ where f is the feature-assignment.

HAS –LABEL , subset of $FN \times Vn'$: (fn_1,y) are in *HAS –LABEL* iff $h(fn_1)=y$, where h is the mapping in Defn. 1.1 (i.e. the attachment of labels to the nodes of the tree in a functional analysis).

IN –ANALYSIS , subset of $FN \times C$: (fn_1,c) are in *IN –ANALYSIS* iff fn_1 is a node in a functional analysis in c.

LEX , subset of $DN \times Vt$: (dn_1,w) are in *LEX* iff dn_1 is a terminal node in the constituent tree and $L(dn_1)=w$ (see Defn. 1.4(d)).

A relationship is also needed to define the hierarchy of functions represented, for each constituent, by its set of functional analyses. The tree-defining relation in Defn. 1.1 is purely local to a single constituent, but for various purposes (in particular the "preselection" realization rule), it is convenient to consider paths of function labels which reach through several constituents. This can be done via the association of function nodes with unit nodes, and the tree structure of the unit nodes. A function node will be associated with a unit node (as in *HAS –FUNCTION* above), that unit node itself has a daughter (defined by *DAUGHTER*), and that daughter will be associated with one or more function nodes. The resulting relation will not define a strict tree, but rather an acyclic graph, as the linking of unit nodes to multiple function nodes does not give a single-parent arrangement:

SUPER , subset of $FN \times FN$: (fn_1,fn_2) are in *SUPER* if fn_1 is the parent of fn_2 in a functional analysis, or if the parent of fn_2 is the root of a functional analysis in a constituent c, and *SAME –NODE* (dn_1,c), and (dn_1,c') is in *DAUGHTER* , (fn_1,c') is in *IN –ANALYSIS* , and (dn_1,fn_1) are in *HAS –FUNCTION* .

The generation process should, on encountering a realization rule, alter the contents of the sets DN, FN, C, and the ten relations described above, to reflect the updated syntactic structure (it is assumed that the whole of F, Vn, and Vt are available throughout). Notice that the ten relations above have been chosen not on the basis of some particular set of realization rules, but because they characterize the essential structural relationships involved in a syntactic structure as defined in §5.1—they form an atomic vocabulary of ways of connecting items, which should suffice to state most reasonable systemic realization rules.

For example, the algorithm for responding to the realization rules given in §5.5 above could be phrased thus, where CC is a variable denoting the constituent currently being built (i.e. the grammatical unit whose features are being accumulated):

$A \char`^ B$: if there are no fn_1, fn_2 in FN, and dn_1, dn_2 in DN such that (fn_1,A) and (fn_2,B) are in $HAS\text{-}LABEL$ and (fn_1,CC), (fn_2,CC) are in $IN\text{-}ANALYSIS$, and (dn_1,fn_1), (dn_2,fn_2) are in $HAS\text{-}FUNCTION$, then create such nodes and entries; ensure that (dn_1,dn_2) are in $NEXT$.

$A(B)$: if there are no fn_1, fn_2 in FN such that (fn_1,A) and (fn_2,B) are in $HAS\text{-}LABEL$, (fn_1,CC), (fn_2,CC) are in $IN\text{-}ANALYSIS$, then create such nodes and entries; ensure that (fn_1,fn_2) are in $SUPER$.

A/B: if there are no fn_1, fn_2 in FN such that (fn_1,A), (fn_2,B) are in $HAS\text{-}LABEL$, and (fn_1,CC), (fn_2,CC) are in $IN\text{-}ANALYSIS$, then create such nodes and entries; ensure that there is a unique node dn_1 in DN such that both (dn_1,fn_1) and (dn_1,fn_2) are in $HAS\text{-}FUNCTION$.

$A = a$: if there is no fn_1 in FN such that (fn_1,A) are in $HAS\text{-}LABEL$, (fn_1,CC) are in $IN\text{-}ANALYSIS$, and dn_1 in DN such that (dn_1,fn_1) are in $HAS\text{-}FUNCTION$, then create such nodes and entries; ensure that (dn_1,a) is in LEX.

$A_1 < A_2 < ... A_m : \alpha$: ensure, by creating new nodes and entries if necessary, that there is a sequence of nodes $fn_1,...fn_m$ in FN and a sequence of nodes $dn_1,...dn_m$ in DN such that:

    (a) dn_1 is in CC
    (b) for all i (2 to m), (dn_i,dn_{i-1}) is in $MOTHER$
    (c) for all i (1 to m), (dn_i,fn_i) is in $HAS\text{-}FUNCTION$
    (d) for all i (1 to m), (fn_i,A_i) is in $HAS\text{-}LABEL$
    (e) (c',α) is in $HAS\text{-}FEATURE$, where $SAME\text{-}NODE(dn_m,c')$

Notice that it is virtually impossible to guarantee that the node-sets and relations formed from the realization rules attached to the various collected features will characterize a completely well-formed structure as defined in §5.1. The grammar-writer has complete freedom to define any realization rules at all, and so could write a grammar which was itself well-formed, but whose derivations produced bizarre or partial syntactic structures.

5.7. Formulating realization rules in logic

In characterizing the notion of a well-formed syntactic structure, a realization rule was said merely to be a mapping from constituents within feature-labelled structures to the set {0,1}; that is, a predicate over structures. A generation algorithm must have a way of using the information in realization rules to define a final structure, building up the information as it proceeds. The approach in §5.6 above (which is based on the implementation described in the next chapter) essentially associates, with each variety of realization rule, a mapping from partial syntactic structures to partial syntactic structures. Hence realization rules are regarded as denoting *two* mappings—the declarative predicate which defines well-formedness of the final structure, and the algorithmic mapping which transforms a partial structure in to another partial structure. It would be more elegant to have a formulation of realization rules which conflates these two uses, allowing a single statement both to act as a predicate over structures and as a recipe for building a structure which conformed to the predicate. This appears to be possible by formalizing the content of realization rules using a first-order logic, so that the generation algorithm manipulates a gradually-increasing set of statements defining the content of the eventual structure.

This approach would involve associating with each realization rule (in a systematic way) a formula of this first-order theory, free in one variable which denotes a constituent. Such a formula can be used to define the mapping from complete syntactic structures to truth-values in a fairly straightforward way (i.e. $Q(x)$ is true of (T, f, c) if $Q(c)$ is true). The same open formulae can be used to build up a structure description gradually, by having the generation procedure transform the formula, for each realization rule it encounters, into a closed formula, by instantiating the free variable to the name of the constituent being built. The final structure is then a well-formed syntactic structure (as in §5.1) which is an interpretation (in the logical sense) of the final set of statements, with the symbolic constants mapped to nodes within the structure and using certain interpretations of predicate symbols (cf. Marcus, Hindle and Fleck, 1983).

For added clarity, this proposal will be outlined using a sorted logic. There are the following basic sorts: daughter nodes, function nodes, constituents, function labels, grammatical features, and lexical items. There are ten predicate names, corresponding to the ten relations defined in §5.6 above, with the obvious interpretations. For instance:

next (X:*daughter—node*, Y:*daughter—node*)—true iff X and Y are in the same constituent and immediately adjacent according to the left-right order.

daughter (X:*daughter—node*, C:*constituent*)—true iff X is in the constituent C.

For example, the realization rules given in §5.5 above could be phrased thus, where X is in each case a free variable of type constituent:

$A \hat{} B$: $\big($Exist $n_1, n_2 : daughter-node$; $fn_1, fn_2 : function-node$ $\big)$ $daughter(n_1, X)$ &
 $daughter(n_2, X)$ & $has-function(n_2, fn_2)$ & $has-label(fn_1, A)$ & $has-label(fn_2, B)$ &
 $next(n_1, n_2)$.

$A(B)$: $\big($Exist $fn_1, fn_2 : function-node$ $\big)$ $super(fn_1, fn_2)$ & $has-label(fn_1, A)$ &
 $has-label(fn_2, B)$ & $in-analysis(fn_1, X)$ & $in-analysis(fn_2, X)$.

A/B : $\big($Exist $n : daughter-node$; $fn_1, fn_2 : function-node$ $\big)$ $daughter(n, X)$ &
 $has-function(n, fn_1)$ & $has-function(n, fn_2)$ & $has-label(fn_1, A)$ & $has-label(fn_2, B)$.

$A = a$: $\big($Exist $n : daughter-node$; $fn_1 : function-node$ $\big)$ $daughter(n, X)$ & $has-function(n, fn_1)$
 & $has-label(fn_1, A)$ & $lex(n, a)$.

$A_1 < A_2 < ... A_m : \alpha$: $\big($Forall $i : 1$ to m $\big)$ $\big($Exist $fn_i : function-node$; $dn_i : daughter-node$;
 $c : constituent$ $\big)$ $mother(dn_i, dn_{i-1})$ & $has-function(dn_i, fn_i)$ & $has-label(fn_i, A_i)$ &
 $daughter(dn_1, X)$ & $same-node(dn_m, c)$ & $has-feature(c, \alpha)$.

As commented in §5.6, there is no guarantee that the structure-description produced by the generator will be coherent. In the formulation in logic, this would show up as a set of realization statements which were inconsistent, or for which there was more than one interpretation.

5.8. Problem reduction

For the purposes of clarification and comparison the generation algorithm can be expressed formally at a higher level of abstraction in terms of "problem reduction." The problem-reduction algorithm (described by Nilsson, 1971, pp. 80-123) involves transforming "problem descriptions" into "reduced" problem descriptions (descriptions of subproblems), through the use of "problem-reduction operators." The objective of the problem-reduction algorithm is to eventually reduce the original problem to a set of primitive problems whose solutions are either trivial or known. A problem-reduction step may reduce a problem to a disjunctive set of subproblems, only one of which must be solved; or a conjunctive set of subproblems, all of which must be solved.

5.8.1. AND/OR graphs

Problem reduction can be illustrated with a graph-like structure. Following Nilsson (ibid.), suppose problem A can be solved either by solving problems B and C, or by solving problems D and E, or by solving problem F. The appropriate AND/OR graph is shown in Figure 5.1 (it is conventional to draw the graph such that each conjunction of subproblems is under its own graph node).

The nodes labelled N and M are introduced as exclusive parents for the sets of subproblems B, C and D, E respectively. If M and N are thought of as acting

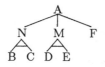

Figure 5.1 (from Nisson).

as problem descriptions, Figure 5.1 shows problem A as having been reduced to any of the alternative subproblems N, M or F. The graph nodes labelled N, M, and F are thus called *OR* nodes. Problem N is reduced to the set of subproblems B and C and these subproblems are represented by *AND* nodes. *AND* nodes are represented by bars between their incoming arcs.

The successors of an *AND/OR* node are either all *OR* nodes or all *AND* nodes (in the case of a single successor there need be no distinction).

Terms such as "parent" node, "successor" node and "arc" connecting two nodes will be used, and given the obvious meaning when discussing *AND/OR* graphs. Each *AND/OR* graph has a single node called the "start node" that represents the initial problem description. Graph nodes corresponding to primitive problem descriptions are called "terminal nodes."

The final objective of the search for an *AND/OR* graph is to show that the start node is "solved." A solved node in an *AND/OR* graph can be defined as follows:

> The terminal nodes are solved nodes (since they are associated with primitive problems)
>
> If a nonterminal node has *OR* successors, then it is a solved node if and only if at least *one* of its successors is solved
>
> If a nonterminal node has *AND* successors, then it is a solved node if and only if *all* of its successors are solved (ibid., p. 89)

The subgraph of solved nodes that demonstrates (according to the definition above) that the start node is solved is defined to be a "solution graph."

5.8.2. System networks and AND/OR graphs
System networks can be interpreted as *AND/OR* graphs, and the processing of the grammar can be interpreted as problem reduction.

Figure 5.2a shows a fragment of a system network. One way of interpreting this network as an *AND/OR* graph is to simply interpret features in systems as

a)   b)

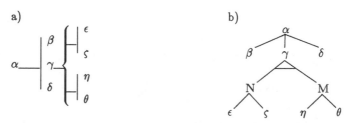

Figure 5.2.

OR nodes (this would really be an *AND /EXCLUSIVE –OR* graph in this case) and
to interpret the curly bracket as specifying *AND* nodes (as shown in Figure 5.2b).
The start node thus corresponds to the least delicate feature in the network. The
informal linguistic interpretation that results, say for the generation of a clause,
is that the problem of generating a *clause* is reduced to either generating a *finite*
clause *OR* a *non-finite* clause, *AND* ..., and the problem of generating a *finite*
clause is reduced to either generating an *imperative* clause or an *indicative* clause
and so on. The systemic text generation system Nigel (see §7.1.2) can be viewed
as taking this approach (§7.4 will compare Nigel and SLANG on the basis of
problem reduction).

     The backward-chaining model characterized by Defn. 3.4 (b) above can also
be interpreted as problem reduction, but here the start node corresponds to a
seed feature not the least delicate feature. The reduction operators are the productions in P_i .

a)   b)

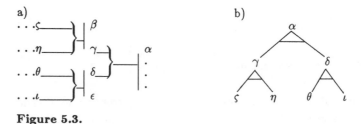

Figure 5.3.

     This interpretation is illustrated in Figure 5.3 where a) shows the network
fragment and b) shows the corresponding *AND /OR* graph. Instead of having one
large *AND /OR* graph stretching from left to right across the entire network,
several smaller *AND /OR* graphs (each starting with a seed feature) stretch from
right to left. Figure 5.3 shows the seed problem α reducing to subproblems γ

AND δ. The problem γ reduces to the problems ς *AND* η, and the problem δ reduces to the problems θ *AND* ι.

It is no coincidence that there are no *OR* nodes in the *AND* /*OR* graph—for this generation relationship problems *always* reduce to *AND* nodes as a result of the stipulation in Defn. 3.4 (b) (i). The two sources of disjunction—systems and disjunctive entry conditions to systems—are resolved implicitly or explicitly by the preselected seed features. Each of the initial seed features in the initial feature set is treated as an initial problem description in this way. The result is that the grammar is spanned from right to left by a number of small *AND* trees. These *AND* trees gradually converge as they stretch left. If one of the subproblems of a particular tree is already part of another tree or subtree, then it is treated as a primitive problem (see above) and not reduced further. Some examples of this convergence are shown in Figures 5.4 and 5.5.

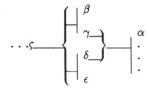

Figure 5.4.

When constructing an *AND* tree for Figure 5.4, the node ς should be attached to γ or δ but not both—once it is attached to one, the other is a primitive problem since the solution is the same for both problems.

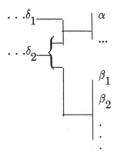

Figure 5.5.

Figure 5.5 shows convergence as a result of disjunction. Suppose the node α is part of an *AND* tree. It may appear that α should be reduced to δ_1 *OR* δ_2. But note that δ_1 is a seed feature by Defn. 4.1, and therefore will be the start node of another *AND* tree. Also note that δ_2 will be part of the *AND* tree of some β_i if it is part of any *AND* tree at all (i.e. if no β_i appears in an *AND* tree—because no features to the right were preselected—then δ_2 can not appear in an *AND* tree without violating Defn. 2.11 (a)). Since both δ_1 and δ_2 must appear in other trees if at all, α should be treated as a primitive problem and not reduced. This is why Defn. 3.4 (b) (which defines the reduction) only reduces features with conjunctive entry conditions.

5.8.3. Backward-chaining and the solution graph

In discussions of problem solving, *AND/OR* graphs are usually explicitly drawn, and the search for the solution consists of searching the graph for a solution graph. In practice however,

> ... we seldom have explicit graphs to search, but instead the graph is defined implicitly by an initial problem description and reduction operators. It is convenient to introduce the notion of a *successor operator* Γ that when applied to a problem description produces all of the sets of successor problem descriptions. (The successor operator Γ is applied by applying all of the applicable reduction operators.) (ibid., p. 90)

In this case, Defn. 2.9 (d) ensures that Γ produces exactly one set of successor problem descriptions—namely those produced by a backward application of "$\Rightarrow$". Note that since Defn. 3.4 (b) results in *AND* nodes only, the solution graph must be exactly the graph defined by Γ.

This section has shown how the processing of system networks can be interpreted in terms of the problem-solving algorithm of problem reduction. This provides a formal model at a higher level of abstraction that can be used to make comparisons between systemic text-generation methods (see §7.4).

5.9. Summary

The linguistic theory of systemic grammar has played, and is likely to continue to play, an important role in text-generation research. A formal model of systemic grammar has been provided in an attempt to make existing ideas more precise. The model includes formal definitions of a systemic grammar, of systemic syntactic structures, and of the language generated by a systemic grammar. The generation method described in Chapter 4 has been expressed within this model as computing a valid feature set from a non-conflicting set of seed features.

Although the formalization given here is largely exploratory, it will hopefully pave the way for a more substantial treatment.

6
The implementation

This chapter will describe the first implementation of the Systemic Linguistic Approach to Natural-language Generation (SLANG-I). SLANG-I has been implemented as a production system using the production language OPS5. Since many OPS5 rules appear in this chapter, a short introduction to OPS5 has been provided in Appendix A.

This chapter is divided into five sections. The first is an overview of the system as a whole. It will provide high-level descriptions and explanations for the mechanisms used in the implementation. The second section is a detailed description of the System Network - OPS5 Rule Translator (SNORT) which outputs the grammar in the form of OPS5 production rules that can be used by SLANG-I. The text-generation system itself—SLANG-I—is described in detail in the third section. The fourth and fifth sections look at the limitations of this implementation and some possible alternatives respectively. Finally, a summary is given.

6.1. Overview

The purpose of this section is to provide a high-level overview of SNORT and SLANG-I before getting down to details in the next two sections. To a large extent this is made necessary by the interdependence between these two components. It is impossible to motivate the output of SNORT before explaining to a certain extent how SLANG-I works, and similarly SLANG-I cannot be explained before it is understood how the grammar is represented in OPS5 production rules. This section consists of four parts: first, a presentation of the abstract architecture of SLANG-I; second, a discussion of the OPS5 productions representing the systemic grammar; third, a description of the data structures used by SLANG-I; and fourth, a brief look at the control strategy used to coordinate the text-generation process.

6.1.1. The abstract architecture

The architecture of SLANG-I is very simple. The primary components are a "problem solver" (the OPS5 inference engine slightly abstracted in the sense that it is being used to do both forward- and backward-chaining—see §6.1.2) and a "knowledge base" (the system networks represented as OPS5 productions). As described in Chapter 4, the problem solver simply forward- and backward-chains using the productions. As the problem solving proceeds, the realization rules attached to those features that are inferred by the problem solver are processed to build a structure realizing the text. It was convenient to process the realization rules with OPS5 productions, so the problem solver also builds the structures. If a more sophisticated problem solver were used in SLANG (e.g. if SLANG were implemented within an expert system) it may also be convenient for the problem solver to build the structure. But note that it is not important whether or not the problem solver performs this task—structure building does not involve search so it does not require the power of the problem solver. So the realization (with the important exception of preselection, which sets goals to be solved) is not really part of the problem solving *per se;* it could just as easily be performed by a simple program.

Thus the abstract architecture is that there are three major components: the problem solver, the knowledge base (grammar), and a mechanism (which in this case happens to be written as productions used by the problem solver) that builds the syntactic structures and outputs the text.

6.1.2. The grammar productions

The previous chapters have already described in abstract terms the forward- and backward-chaining rules which are the SLANG interpretation of gates and system features respectively. To avoid confusion with these abstract rules, and also with realization rules, the term "production" will be used instead of "rule" when referring to OPS5 code.

The forward-chaining rules (gates) can be implemented as OPS5 productions in a very straightforward manner. Working memory elements of the form (chosen x) can represent the fact that feature x has been chosen. The left-hand side (LHS) of the production simply specifies the logical combination of features acting as the entry conditions of the gate. The right-hand side (RHS) puts an element of the form (chosen ...) in working memory indicating that the feature has been chosen, and puts a "realization statement" in working memory for each realization rule of the gate ("realization statement" is used for the OPS5 version of a systemic realization rule). For instance the feature *non-bene-reception*

$$
\left.\begin{array}{l}
\text{. . .non-benefactive}\_ \\[1em]
\text{. . .receptive}_____
\end{array}\right\}\_\_\_\_\text{non-bene-reception} \atop \text{\small Medium / Subject}
$$

can be written in OPS5 as

```
;;;IF    the features non-benefactive and receptive have been chosen
;;;THEN    choose non-bene-reception and conflate Medium and Subject
(p non-bene-reception::first-approx
  (chosen non-benefactive)
  (chosen receptive)
-->
  (make chosen non-bene-reception)
  (make conflate ^fun Medium ^with Subject))
```

Ideally, backward-chaining rules could be implemented similarly, with the entry conditions in the LHS, realization statements in the RHS, and a (make chosen ...) statement also in the RHS. Then if there was a goal to choose such a feature, the realization rules would be treated as effects, and the entry conditions would be set as subgoals. Note that this would involve looking at the RHS of productions to determine which productions satisfy the goal. Unfortunately, the OPS5 architecture—technically speaking—is strictly forward-chaining; productions are selected solely on the basis of matching the LHS with working memory.

This problem can be overcome by using working memory elements of the form (goal x) and writing productions so the goal statement is matched in the LHS (e.g. Brownston et al., 1985, Appendix). The entry conditions must be made into subgoals in the RHS. For instance:

```
;;;IF   there is a goal to choose declarative
;;;THEN   change the goal statement to a chosen statement,
;;;      and set indicative as a subgoal,
;;;      and make the Subject adjacent to the Finite element
(p declarative::first-approx
  (goal declarative)
-->
  (modify 1 ^1 chosen)
  (make goal indicative)
  (make adjacent ^to Subject ^is Finite))
```

Thus backward-chaining can be implemented within the OPS5 forward-chaining architecture. Notice this prevents the realization relationships being stated as goals (e.g. there can be no goal to make the Agent the Theme as in §4.2.2; the original goals are all preselected features as in §4.2.5).

Although all OPS5 productions are—in the strictly technical sense—forward-chaining, the terms "forward-chaining production" and "backward-chaining production" will be used to refer to productions that represent the abstract forward- and backward-chaining rules described in Chapter 4.

Another problem resulting from OPS5 is that several identical elements in working memory will independently match the LHS of productions. This may cause a production to fire several times, perhaps generating more redundant working memory elements. For instance, several features have *declarative* as an entry condition. If each one puts a separate (goal declarative) in working memory, the production above will fire several times, generating several copies of (goal indicative), which in turn will cause the production for *indicative* to fire several times (in addition to all the redundant firings as a resulting from *it* being an entry condition to several features) and so on. A similar phenomenon occurs when gates have disjunctive entry conditions. If several of the disjuncts are satisfied, the production will fire for each one—resulting in several firings of productions whose LHS matches the identical copies of the "chosen" statement and so on.

This accumulation of redundant work for the problem solver is unacceptable. The solution to this problem adopted here is to call a LISP operator, which checks if a feature has been chosen already before it creates a new "goal" or "chosen" statement. These operators are called GOAL and ASSERT respectively and are used throughout the implementation instead of "make goal" and "make chosen" respectively.

```
;;;IF    there is a goal to choose declarative
;;;THEN   choose declarative, set indicative as a subgoal,
;;;       and make the Subject adjacent to the Finite element
(p declarative::second-approx
  (goal declarative)
-->
  (modify 1 ^1 chosen)
  (call GOAL indicative)
  (make adjacent ^to Subject ^is Finite))
```

6.1.3. The syntactic structures

The productions just described represent realization rules using OPS5 realization statements that are put into working memory. A substantial part of the SLANG-I system consists of OPS5 productions whose LHS matches these realization statements. The RHS of each of these productions modifies the structure of the text accordingly. These realization productions are described in detail later; the point that needs to be made here is that the structure being built plays an important role in the text generation.

The building block for the linguistic structures is the "hub" (from Mann et al., 1983). A hub is represented by a unique atom—generated by LISP's "gensym" or OPS5's "genatom." Recall from Chapter 5 that the structure has the form of a constituent tree. The hubs are the nodes in this tree. Each hub is associated with, *inter alia,* a set of functions (Agent, Subject, etc.). The hubs themselves do not have individual entries in working memory, but merely appear in the individual entries for each of the associated functions. Each function has an entry in working memory with the following template:

```
(hub ^of      [e.g. Subject, Head, !Noun etc.]
     ^is      [the hub identifier e.g. g00023]
     ^super   [another hub e.g. g00005]
     ^output? [either yes, no, or nil]
     ^lex     [e.g. ran, John, in etc.]
     ^mom     [another hub e.g. g00007]
)
```

Note the correspondence between some of these fields and the formal description of the structure in the previous chapter.

If two functions are conflated, for instance the Subject and the Agent, the descriptions will be changed so that they have the same ^is field (i.e. they have the same hub): e.g. (hub ^of Subject ^is g00015...), (hub ^of Agent ^is g00015...). The ^super field describes hierarchies of functions as defined by the expansion realization rule. For instance the Subject and the Finite are both subfunctions of the Mood, hence the hub of the Mood will appear in the ^super field of both the Subject and Finite, e.g.:

> (hub ^of Finite ^is g00056 ^super g00023...)
> (hub ^of Subject ^is g00043 ^super g00023...)
> (hub ^of Mood ^is g00023...)

Similarly, the ^mom field contains the hub of the next *unit* above in the structure hierarchy. For instance if the Subject in a clause is realized by a nominal-group, all the functions in that nominal-group will have the hub of the Subject in their ^mom field. If the Head of that nominal-group is realized at the word rank by a noun, the function in the noun network (there is only one—!Noun) will have the Head of the nominal-group in its ^mom field.

All this leads up to an important point: there may be several nominal-groups in, for instance, a clause, and it is not good enough to put (chosen determined) in working memory without indicating to which of the nominal-groups it refers. If both the Subject and the Medium of a particular clause are realized by nominal-groups, and (hub ^of Subject ^is g00016 ^mom g00005) and (hub ^of Medium ^is g00018 ^mom g00005) and the Subject is determined, then (chosen determined g00016) will unambiguously state this fact. A similar addition must be made to "goal" statements and realization statements. The final form of a forward-chaining production, for instance *non-bene-reception*, is:

```
;;;IF   the features non-benefactive and receptive have been chosen
;;;THEN   choose non-bene-reception and conflate Medium and Subject
(p non-bene-reception
  (chosen non-benefactive <mom>)
  (chosen receptive <mom>)
-->
  (call ASSERT chosen non-bene-reception <mom>)
  (make conflate ^fun Medium ^with Subject ^mom <mom>))
```

6.1.4. The control strategy

Before the final form for backward-chaining productions can be given, one last issue must be resolved: the control strategy. It is desirable to have the text generated in a left-to-right fashion so it can be output as it is generated. This is accomplished by marking the hubs in the structure as "sub-judice" (under consideration), in a left-to-right depth-first manner, and not firing backward-chaining productions unless they are relevant to hubs in a "sub-judice" statement in working memory.

```
;;;IF   there is a goal to choose declarative at a node under consideration
;;;THEN   choose declarative, set indicative as a subgoal,
;;;      and make the Subject adjacent to the Finite element
(p declarative
  (sub-judice <mom>)
  (goal declarative <mom>)
-->
  (modify 2 ^1 chosen)
  (call GOAL indicative <mom>)
  (make adjacent ^to Subject ^is Finite ^mom <mom>))
```

Since forward-chaining productions are dependent on features chosen by backward-chaining productions, only the latter need an explicit check.

6.1.5. Overview conclusion

This overview has provided a high-level gloss of the workings of SLANG-I and motivation for the form of the productions representing the grammar. The next section will describe in detail how these productions are generated automatically from a system network notation. The section following that will describe the details of SLANG-I including the productions for realization, and productions for implementing the control strategy and output.

6.2. SNORT (System Network - OPS5 Rule Translator)

The implementation of SLANG-I depends on the systemic grammar being in the form of OPS5 productions. To this end a set of LISP operators has been written that translates from a system-network-like notation to OPS5 productions (the System Network - OPS5 Rule Translator: SNORT). This section will briefly describe this translation and the program that performs it.

6.2.1. The system network notation

Since it is impractical to enter grammars in the graphical notation in which they appear in the linguistic literature, some notation must be used that can easily be input using ordinary keyboards and characters. The solution to this problem is a LISP based notation which represents the grammar feature-by-feature, but which also attempts to capture some of the graphics through the use of symbols such as -{=,]-, =}- and so on. The idea was not to create a notation that the grammar-writer can use to develop the system networks, but rather to create a notation that the grammar-writer could easily use to type in his system networks once they have been developed. It is intended that the grammar-writer modifies and expands the grammar while referring to the original graphical notation, and then enters these changes using the LISP notation.

First, consider the gates or forward-chaining rules. These are represented as lists (EC f RR1 RR2 ...) where the first element of the list is a description of the entry conditions, the second element is the name of the feature, and any further elements are realization rules. The description of an entry condition is a list where the the final element is a graphical symbol and the other elements are either features or nested descriptions of entry conditions. The graphical symbols =}- and -<> represent conjunction, the symbol]- represents disjunction, and the symbols -- and -{= are used when there is only one feature acting as the entry condition.

Here are some examples:

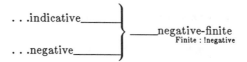

is written

((indicative negative =}-) negative-finite
    (Finite : !negative)).

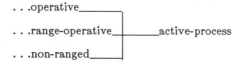

is written

((operative range-operative non-ranged]-) active-process).

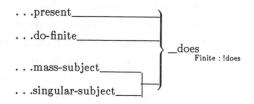

is written

```
((present
  do-finite
  (mass-subject singular-subject ]-)
=}-) does
    (Finite : !does))
```

Note that the nesting can be arbitrarily complex with ordinary LISP parentheses indicating the nesting. For instance the gate shown in Figure 6.1a is written as shown in Figure 6.1b.

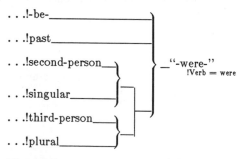

Figure 6.1a.

The "diamond" notation which is often used to avoid tangled system networks has also been implemented.

Part A) of Figure 6.2 uses the bracket notation which requires crossed lines. Features *e* and *f* are represented in this case by ((a c =}-) e) and ((a d =}-) f) respectively. Part B) of Figure 6.2 uses the diamond notation to avoid the crossed lines. In this case the same features are represented by ((a c -<>) e)

```
(((!-be-
  !past
  ((!second-person !singular =}-)
   (!third-person !plural =}-)
  ]-)
 =}-) "-were-"
     (!Verb = were))
```

Figure 6.1b.

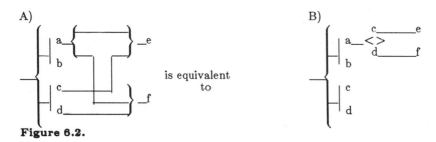

Figure 6.2.

and ((a d -<>) f). Note that in the LISP notation =}- and -<> are synonymous.

Features that are terms in systems are represented in much the same way as features that are gates. The graphical symbol -[is used to represent a system.

As in the case of gates, complex entry conditions are simply nested. The following system from Winograd (1983, p. 293)

can be written as three statements—one for each feature:

(((third singular =}-) -[) feminine)
(((third singular =}-) -[) masculine)
(((third singular =}-) -[) neuter)

Labelling of systems (e.g. GENDER above) is a common practice, and often provides useful documentation. Thus the notation allows the system labels, in capitals, to appear in place of the entry condition to the system. The above system can also be written:

((third singular =}-) GENDER)
((GENDER -[) masculine)
((GENDER -[) feminine)
((GENDER -[) neuter)

Often there is a single feature acting as a particular entry condition. The graphical symbols used to represent this are -- and -{=. The difference between these is purely visual; the latter is used if a branch appears in the system network. The network shown in Figure 6.3a would be written as shown in Figure 6.3b.

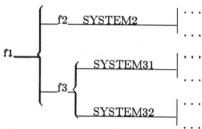

Figure 6.3a.

((f1 -{=) f2)
  ((f2 --) SYSTEM2)
    ((SYSTEM2 -[) ...)
    ((SYSTEM2 -[) ...)
((f1 -{=) f3)
  ((f3 -{=) SYSTEM31)

  .

  .

  ((f3 -{=) SYSTEM32)

  .

  .

Figure 6.3b.

As another example:

114

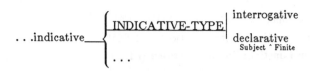

is written:

((indicative -{=) INDICATIVE-TYPE)
((INDICATIVE-TYPE -[) declarative (Subject ˆ Finite))
((INDICATIVE-TYPE -[) interrogative)

6.2.2. The production rule notation

The system network notation is translated by SNORT into OPS5 (Forgey, 1981; Brownston, et al., 1985) production rules. There are two production templates that are used, one for forward-chaining and one for backward-chaining. The forward-chaining productions have the form:

```
(p feature-name
  (chosen entry-condition1 <mom>)
  (chosen entry-condition2 <mom>)
        .
        .
        .
  (chosen entry-conditionN <mom>)
-->
  (call ASSERT chosen feature-name <mom>)
  (make realization-statement1 ˆmom <mom>)
  (make realization-statement2 ˆmom <mom>)
        .
        .
        .
  (make realization-statementN ˆmom <mom>))
```

The entry conditions illustrated in this template are conjuncts. If there is disjunction within the conjuncts, OPS5 disjunction << d1 d2 d3 ... dn >> is used to represent this. Also, the realization statements are written in the OPS5 attribute-value notation. These take one of the following forms (equivalent rule form in parentheses):

adjacent ^to Function1 ^is Function2 (F1 ^ F2)

expand ^fun Function1 ^into Function2 (F1(F2))

conflate ^fun Function1 ^with Function2 (F1 / F2)

lexify ^fun Function1 ^as lex1 (F1 = lex1)

preselect ^feature feature1 ^for Function1 ... FunctionN

(F1<F2...<FN : f)

For instance the forward-chaining rule *does* illustrated above is written:

```
;;;IF    present, do-finite, and mass- or singular-subject has been chosen
;;;THEN   choose does and preselect the lexical feature
;;;      !does for the Finite element
 (p does
   (chosen present <mom>)
   (chosen do-finite <mom>)
   (chosen << mass-subject singular-subject >> <mom>)
  -->
   (call ASSERT chosen does <mom>)
   (make preselect ^feature !does ^for Finite ^mom <mom>))
```

The forward-chaining rule for *active-process*

is written:

```
;;;IF    operative, range-operative or non-ranged has been chosen
;;;THEN   choose active-process
 (p active-process
   (chosen << operative range-operative non-ranged >> <mom>)
  -->
   (call ASSERT chosen active-process <mom>))
```

At this point a complication is encountered. Recall the gate "-were-" above. It contains conjunction nested within the disjunction. This was no problem for the LISP notation, but it poses a problem for the simple OPS5 templates described above. In OPS5 there is no way to express conjunction nested within disjunction in this way. The solution is not difficult however: intermediate productions can be introduced such that there is only one level of conjunction in any

116

one production. In the case of "-were-", for instance, the problem is conjoining *!second-person* and *!singular* within a disjunct, and *!third-person* and *!singular* in another disjunct. If two intermediate productions are written (using the same template illustrated above):

```
;;;IF   !second-person and !singular have been chosen
;;;THEN   choose the dummy feature "-were-"g00005
 (p "-were-"g00005
   (chosen !second-person <mom>)
   (chosen !singular <mom>)
 -->
   (call ASSERT chosen "-were-"g00005 <mom>))
```

and

```
;;;IF   !third-person and !plural have been chosen
;;;THEN   choose the dummy feature "-were-"g00006
 (p "-were-"g00006
   (chosen !third-person <mom>)
   (chosen !plural <mom>)
 -->
   (call ASSERT chosen "-were-"g00006 <mom>))
```

then the forward-chaining production can be written as

```
;;;IF   one of the dummy features "-were-"g00005 or "-were-"g00006
;;;     have been chosen as well as !-be- and !past
;;;THEN   choose "-were-" and assign !Verb the lexical item "were".
 (p "-were-"
   (chosen !-be- <mom>)
   (chosen !past <mom>)
   (chosen << "-were-"g00005 "-were-"g00006 >> <mom>)
 -->
   (call ASSERT chosen "-were-" <mom>)
   (make lexify ^fun !Verb ^as were ^mom <mom>))
```

Since an arbitrary number of intermediate levels of productions can be introduced (recursively, as described below), arbitrarily complex entry conditions can be handled.

The backward-chaining productions have, of course, a different template:

```
(p feature-name
  (sub-judice <mom>)
  (goal feature-name <mom>)
-->
  (modify 2 ^1 chosen)
  (call GOAL entry-condition1 <mom>)
  (call GOAL entry-condition2 <mom>)
            .
            .
            .
  (call GOAL entry-conditionN <mom>)
  (make realization-rule1 ^mom <mom>)
  (make realization-rule2 ^mom <mom>)
            .
            .
            .
  (make realization-ruleN ^mom <mom>))
```

As one would expect, the production is activated if the particular feature is a goal, the entry conditions are set as subgoals, and the realization statements are the effects. The "modify 2 ^1 chosen" means "modify the first field of the second condition to 'chosen'" so that the "goal" statement is now a "chosen" statement. The "sub-judice" at the beginning of the production is for controlling the order of execution of the productions, and will be explained later. For instance:

```
;;;IF   there is a goal to choose declarative at a sub-judice node
;;;THEN   choose declarative, set indicative as a subgoal,
;;;       and make the Subject adjacent to the Finite element
  (p declarative
    (sub-judice <mom>)
    (goal declarative <mom>)
  -->
    (modify 2 ^1 chosen)
    (call GOAL indicative <mom>)
    (make adjacent ^to Subject ^is Finite ^mom <mom>))
```

It is possible to have complex entry conditions to systems, and it would be easy enough to use intermediate productions to handle nested conjunction, as in the case of gates. But recall (from §4.2.5) that disjunctive conditions pose a special problem to backward-chaining—this was the reason that independent disjuncts needed to be included as seed features.

Generally, when a disjunctive entry condition is encountered during backward-chaining, it amounts to a choice. The question is: along which path does the best solution lie? Indeed, the wrong choice could lead to a conflict and to backtracking. Faced with disjunctive entry conditions, even goal-directed backward-chaining degenerates to searching explicitly through alternatives.

Fortunately, in many search spaces—including those normally represented by systemic grammars—there is a high degree of interdependence between the various branches of the search path. This can be exploited by the technique of *least commitment* (Stefik et al., 1983b, pp. 106-110). Least commitment suggests that when a disjunctive entry condition is encountered, the choice should just be left pending since it is very likely that one of the disjuncts will appear in the solution to another goal, thus gratuitously resolving the pending disjunction *without choice*. In systemic terms, if there are several possible entry conditions to a goal feature, the choice should be delayed. If one of the entry conditions is chosen as part of another backward-chain of reasoning, then there is no longer any problem—the entry conditions of the goal feature are satisfied.

Generally, there will always be the possibility that none of the disjuncts ever appear gratuitously, in which case some form of search must take place. The policy in SLANG-I is for the semantic stratum to provide enough knowledge so that there is no blind search whatsoever. The case where search would be needed is exactly the case of independent disjuncts, and the avoidance of this search is the reason that independent disjuncts are preselected. Thus the resolution of disjunctive entry conditions is guaranteed. For this reason it was decided to simplify SLANG-I by not implementing least commitment at all—disjunctive entry conditions are simply ignored entirely. This does not affect the forward- and backward-chaining since the disjunction would always be resolved gratuitously by a preselected feature or by another chain of reasoning.

$((((a\ b\ ]-)\ c =\}-)\ -[)$ sample)

would be translated into

```
(p sample
 (sub-judice <mom>)
 (goal sample <mom>)
-->
 (modify 2 ^1 chosen)
 (call GOAL c <mom>))
```

assuming that either *a* or *b* will be preselected or chosen when achieving another goal. This is a simplifying assumption made in this implementation. If a more sophisticated problem solver were used, it would explicitly use least commitment and would perform the appropriate checks.

6.2.3. The translation

The top level operator of SNORT (see Patten, 1986, §D.5), takes as an argument a list of feature descriptions as described above. It simply loops through this list, translating each feature (skipping over the system labels—identified by being in capitals) into OPS5 productions. For each feature, the operator "f-p" (feature to production) is called with the following arguments:

a) the feature name,

b) a flag indicating whether or not the feature is "in a system" (i.e. a term in a system, or an entry condition to a feature "in a system"—this determines whether the feature is written as a forward- or backward-chaining production),

c) the entry conditions to the system. (Note that the entry conditions of a system will not be specified in the same feature description as the feature name if a system label is used. In this case SNORT simply finds the description for the system label, and uses the entry conditions there. For instance, the entry condition of *masculine* in its feature description is GENDER. So the description of GENDER is found, and the entry conditions—*third* and *singular*—are used in the production for *masculine*.)

d) a list of the realization rules.

"F-p" simply builds a production following one of the two templates (depending on the "in-a-system" flag). There are two important operators that are called by "f-p": "decode," which decodes the entry condition description; and "unformat," which translates the systemic format realization rules into realization statements in the OPS5 attribute-value notation.

Decode takes the nested entry condition descriptions described above (including =}-, -[, -<> etc.) and returns a list of conjuncts where any sublists are disjuncts (there is no further nesting). Thus "f-p" can easily take this and write each element of the list as a condition in the case of gates, or ignore the disjuncts in the case of systems. Thus it is "decode" that is responsible for building the intermediate productions for gates with nested conjunction in their entry conditions. This is done very easily, however, by simply calling "f-p" with trivial arguments (where the name of the intermediate production is made by concatenating the original feature name with a unique symbol returned by gensym). Since "f-p" and "decode" are mutually recursive in this way, arbitrary levels of nesting can be handled.

The other important operator called by "f-p" is "unformat." In most cases the unformatting of realization rules is trivial. For instance, if the argument is

"(F1 / F2)," "unformat" returns "(make conflate ^fun F1 ^with F2 ^mom <mom>)." The only difficult case is preselection. The rule "(Goal<Deictic<Head : !singular)," is unformatted to "(preselect ^feature !singular ^for Goal Deictic Head ^mom <mom>)" where "Goal Deictic Head" is a path describing the place in structure to which the feature applies.

Aside from a few subtleties, in particular the creation of intermediate productions, SNORT is a very simple program. The top-level operator takes a second argument, a file name, and the resulting OPS5 productions are pretty-printed to this file. Once the system network has been SNORTed, the productions can be loaded into OPS5 any number of times. SNORT only needs to be used again if changes are made to the network.

6.3. SLANG-I

The first implementation of the "Systemic Linguistic Approach to Natural-language Generation" generates text using the the OPS5 productions output by SNORT. Aside from SNORT, the rest of the system can be divided into two parts: first, the linguistic productions that interpret the realization statements and build the structure of the text; second, the non-linguistic productions and operators responsible for the low-level workings of the system. These will be discussed in the following two sections.

6.3.1. Realization productions

This section describes the OPS5 realization productions, which interpret the realization statements put in working memory during the processing of the grammar. These productions are responsible for building a linguistic structure for the text being generated.

OPS5 grammar productions use the "make" command to put elements in working memory. The first three productions look for realization statements in working memory that involve functions which do not yet have function descriptions. In each case a function description is created with the "make" command, and a unique hub is created using the built-in OPS5 function "genatom." Remember when reading the OPS5 productions that only those fields relevant to the pattern matching process will appear in the LHS of the production, and that the attribute-value pairs may appear in any order.

```
;;;IF   there is a conflate, lexify or expand statement
;;;     whose first argument does not have a hub,
;;;THEN   create a unique hub for it.
(p new-hub::first-arg
  (<< conflate lexify expand >> ^fun <f> ^mom <m>)
 -(hub ^of <f> ^mom <m>)
-->
  (make hub ^of <f> ^is (genatom) ^mom <m>))
```

```
;;;IF   there is a conflate statement whose second
;;;     argument does not have a hub,
;;;THEN   create a unique hub for it.
(p new-hub::second-arg:conflate
  (conflate ^with <f> ^mom <m>)
 -(hub ^of <f> ^mom <m>)
-->
  (make hub ^of <f> ^is (genatom) ^mom <m>))
```

```
;;;IF   there is an expand statement whose second
;;;     argument does not have a hub,
;;;THEN   create a unique hub for it.
(p new-hub::second-arg:expand
  (expand ^into <f> ^mom <m>)
 -(hub ^of <f> ^mom <m>)
-->
  (make hub ^of <f> ^is (genatom) ^mom <m>))
```

For instance, suppose a conflation statement is put in working memory during the processing of the grammar:

(conflate ^fun Subject ^with Agent ^mom g00007)

Furthermore, suppose neither of these functions appears in any of the realization statements processed at this particular point in structure—and thus they do not yet have hubs assigned to them. Note that the first condition of the first production is matched by this conflation statement (conflate ^fun Subject ^mom g00007), and *ex hypothesi* the second condition is met since there is no working memory element (hub ^of Subject ^mom g00007). Thus the first production can fire, resulting in (for instance)

(hub ^of Subject ^is g00010 ^mom g00007)

being added to working memory. Similarly, the second production also matches (conflate ˆwith Agent ˆmom g00007), and since there is no (hub ˆof Agent ˆmom g00007) this production can also fire adding (for instance)

(hub ˆof Agent ˆis g00011 ˆmom g00007)

to working memory. For the actual conflation see the description below.

Hubs are created in a similar manner for functions appearing in lexify and expand statements. Preselection and adjacency are both special cases. Recall that preselection statements can contain an arbitrary number of functions in the paths. Thus it is easiest to write a special production for preselection that calls LISP to loop through the list of functions in the path (see below). Adjacency is special because it does not require changes in the function descriptions (note that there is no ˆadjacent attribute for the functions). In fact the adjacency statements put in working memory by the grammar are simply used as they stand.

The OPS5 productions that actually interpret the realization rules of the grammar can now be described. These productions will not fire until hubs have been created for all functions involved in the productions above. The first production is for expansion:

```
;;;IF    an expand statement is encountered,
;;;       expanding a function into subfunctions
;;;THEN   put the hub of the expanded function as the ˆsuper
;;;       of the hub of the subfunction.
(p expand
  {(expand ˆfun <f> ˆinto <subf> ˆmom <m>)     <expand>}
  (hub ˆof <f> ˆis <h> ˆmom <m>)
  {(hub ˆof <subf> ˆmom <m>)                    <hub-of-subf>}
  -->
  (modify <hub-of-subf> ˆsuper <h>)
  (remove <expand>))
```

This is a very simple production that simply inserts a value for ˆsuper into the subfunction's description. For instance, if (expand ˆfun Mood ˆinto Subject ˆmom g00012) and (hub ˆof Subject ˆsuper nil ˆmom g00012) and (hub ˆof Mood ˆis g00004 ˆmom g00012) are all in working memory, then the description of Subject will be modified to (hub ˆof Subject ˆsuper g00004 ˆmom g00012).

The "conflate" production itself simply recognizes the need for a conflation and then sets a task that will be performed by another set of productions.

```
;;;IF    a conflate statement is encountered and the functions
;;;      have different hubs,
;;;THEN   substitute the hub of the first for all instances
;;;      of the hub of the second by setting the task change-hub.
(p conflate
  {(conflate ^fun <f1> ^with <f2> ^mom <m>)    <conflate>}
  (hub ^of <f1> ^is <h1> ^mom <m>)
  (hub ^of <f2> ^is { <h2> <> <h1> } ^mom <m>)
-->
  (remove <conflate>)
  (make task change-hub <h2> to <h1>))
```

For instance, if the conflation statement (conflate ^fun Subject ^with Agent ^mom g00007) and (hub ^of Subject ^is g00010 ^mom g00007) and (hub ^of Agent ^is g00011 ^mom g00007) are all in working memory, then the element (task change-hub g00011 to g00010) is put in working memory, activating the following set of productions:

```
;;;IF    any functions are associated with the old hub,
;;;THEN   associate them with the new one instead.
(p change-hub::functions
  (task change-hub <old> to <new>)
  {(hub ^is <old>)                                <hub>}
-->
  (modify <hub> ^is <new>))
```

The above production is useful in cases where there are several functions associated with the to-be-replaced hub (as a result of previous conflations).

```
;;;IF    any attribute-value statements have the old hub in the ^mom field,
;;;THEN   change it to the new one.
(p change-hub::mothers:value-attribute
  (task change-hub <old> to <new>)
  {(<< hub adjacent >> ^mom <old>)                <hub/adjacent>}
-->
  (modify <hub/adjacent> ^mom <new>))
```

```
;;;IF    any vector statements have the old hub in the last (mom) field,
;;;THEN   change it to the new one.
(p change-hub::mothers:vector
  (task change-hub <old> to <new>)
  {(<< chosen goal >> {} <old>)                   <vector>}
-->
  (modify <vector> ^3 <new>))
```

```
;;;IF    any ^super fields have the old hub
;;;THEN   change it to the new one.
(p change-hub::super
   (task change-hub <old> to <new>)
   {(hub ^super <old>)                                    <hub>}
 -->
   (modify <hub> ^super <new>))
```

The task "change-hub" has the effect of simply substituting the new hub symbol for the old one throughout working memory.

The production for lexification, like that for expansion, simply adds a value to a field in the function description—in this case the ^lex field.

```
;;;IF   a lexify statement is encountered,
;;;THEN    associate the lexical item with the function's hub.
(p lexify
   {(lexify ^fun <f> ^as <lex> ^mom <m>)                  <lexify>}
   {(hub ^of <f> ^is <h> ^mom <m> ^output? <> yes)        <hub>}
 -->
   (modify <hub> ^lex <lex> ^output? no)
   (remove <lexify>))
```

The only moderately difficult realization is preselection. Here the difficulty is not because preselection itself is especially complex, but merely because the paths in preselection involve a variable number of functions, and therefore are not easily handled directly by the OPS5 pattern-matching facility.

However, OPS5 allows LISP operators to be called from the RHS of productions.

```
;;;IF   a preselection statement is encountered
;;;THEN   pass the whole thing to a LISP operator that handles this.
;;;      [This is necessary because the number of arguments is arbitrary.]
(p preselect
   {(preselect ^feature <feature> ^mom <m>)       <preselect>}
 -->
   (call PRESELECT (substr <preselect> 1 inf))
   (remove <preselect>))
```

The LISP operator PRESELECT (see Patten, 1986, §D.4) receives a feature and a path (list of functions) as arguments. It loops through the list of functions where each function appears in the ^mom field of the next function in the list (if necessary, a new hub and function description are created). Finally, a goal statement for the feature is put in working memory, with the mother corresponding to the last element in the list.

Suppose a preselection statement is put in working memory during the processing of the grammar: (preselect ˆfeature !feminine ˆfor Agent Deictic Head ˆmom g00006). Suppose none of these functions have hubs already. PRESELECT is called and begins looping through the list (Agent Deictic Head). The Agent in this case is a function at the current place in structure, so an element such as (hub ˆof Agent ˆis h00004 ˆmom g00006) is created with the help of gensym. The further elements (hub ˆof Deictic ˆis h00005 ˆmom h00004) and (hub ˆof Head ˆis h00006 ˆmom h00005) are then created. Thus the path as a whole points to the place in structure occupied by the hub h00006. Accordingly, an element (goal !feminine h00006) is placed in working memory to actually perform the preselection.

6.3.2. The support system

The other group of productions to be described are those responsible for the low-level workings of the system. These productions are concerned with two related aspects of the system. The productions are responsible for keeping track of what parts of the text have been output. Also, most of the productions are used to coordinate the system so that the text is generated from left to right.

The first production can be found in almost any OPS5 program:

```
;;;IF    a task is no longer appropriate
;;;      [it matches no other productions],
;;;THEN    delete it.
(p remove-task
  {(task)                                      <task>}
  -->
  (remove <task>))
```

OPS5 will match statements with more specific (more vector places specified) conditions first; since this condition is the least specific possible, it is guaranteed to match last, that is when the task has already been done (see Waltzman, 1983, p. 29).

The next production is used to mark functions conflated with an output function as also being output.

```
;;;IF   a hub has been output,
;;;THEN   ensure hub's wm elements are marked accordingly.
(p spread-output
   (hub ^is <h> ^output? yes)
   {(hub ^is <h> ^output? < > yes)                <out-of-date>}
   -->
   (modify <out-of-date> ^output? yes))
```

The remaining productions involve the idea of a node being sub-judice, or under consideration. The idea is that nodes in the structure are marked as being sub-judice progressively from left to right as more of the text is actually output. Recall that the backward-chaining productions in the grammar require the place in structure (the mother node) to be sub-judice before they can fire. Thus when the nominal-group realizing the leftmost constituent in a clause (say the Topical) is sub-judice, productions for this nominal-group will fire first. The sub-judice "marker" is only moved to the right once the constituents to the left have actually been output. Of course it is slightly more complicated than this because the structure is a graph resembling a tree, not a list. Since OPS5 gives the most recent working-memory elements priority, if the structure graph is created depth-first, the deepest element has the highest priority, but the ancestors are also sub-judice. So going back to the previous example, the productions will fire for the nominal-group if possible, but if there have not been enough preselections, the generation of the Topical will eventually get stuck. The next most recent node (the clause) then has some more of *its* productions fired until a preselection or conflation (e.g. Topical / Subject) gives the nominal-group productions some more information to work with. Thus in general, the sub-judice constraint forces the generation to proceed in an in-order depth-first manner.

It may appear that there is a possibility of the generation getting "deadlocked" if a preselection is required from a non-sub-judice node. It becomes clear that deadlock can not occur, however, when it is considered that the only source of input to the generation at a particular node is preselection, and preselection can only come from an ancestor in the constituent tree, and all ancestors of a sub-judice node are required to be sub-judice themselves. Therefore, because preselection is directional, deadlock cannot occur.

The following production is a result of the possibility of a hub having more than one supernode. For instance, if the Topical is conflated with the Subject (a common occurrence), then the common hub will be a subnode of both the Theme (the supernode of Topical) and Mood (the supernode of the Subject). This production ensures that if the Subject is sub-judice by virtue of being conflated with the Topical, then the Mood should also be sub-judice.

```
;;;IF   a node is under-consideration (sub-judice),
;;;THEN   make sure any supernodes are also under consideration.
(p fill-scope::super
  (sub-judice <sj>)
  (hub ^is <sj> ^super { <super> <> nil })
  –(sub-judice <super>)
  -->
  (make sub-judice <super>))
```

The following production actually outputs a lexical item. If a hub is sub-judice and it has a lexical item associated with it (see lexify above) then simply write out the lexical item and mark the hub as output.

```
;;;IF   a lexical item has been associated with a hub,
;;;     and that hub is sub-judice,
;;;THEN   output that lexical item and mark the hub as output.
(p output
  {(hub ^is <h> ^lex { <l> <> nil } ^output? no)         <hub>}
  (sub-judice <h>)
  -->
  (write <l> (crlf))
  (modify <hub> ^output? yes))
```

The final set of productions is responsible for the flow of control through the structure network. The first of these productions moves the sub-judice marker down one level of unit nesting.

```
;;;IF   a node is sub-judice and not output,
;;;THEN   declare its leftmost child (if there is one) sub-judice.
(p move::down:#
  (sub-judice <sj>)
  (adjacent ^to # ^is <f> ^mom <sj>)
  (hub ^of <f> ^is <h> ^output? <> yes ^mom <sj>)
  –(hub ^is <sj> ^output? yes)
  -->
  (make sub-judice <h>))
```

The second production moves the sub-judice marker down to the leftmost subnode of a node that is sub-judice.

```
;;;IF   a node is sub-judice and not output,
;;;THEN   declare its leftmost subnode (if there is one) sub-judice.
(p move::down:%
  (sub-judice <sj>)
  (adjacent ^to % ^is <f> ^mom <m>)
  (hub ^of <f> ^is <h> ^super <sj> ^output? <> yes ^mom <m>)
  −(hub ^is <sj> ^output? yes)
  -->
  (make sub-judice <h>))


;;;IF   a hub has just been output
;;;THEN   declare the node adjacent to it (if there is one) sub-judice.
(p move::across
  (hub ^of <f> ^output? yes ^mom <m>)
  (adjacent ^to <f> ^is <f1> ^mom <m>)
  (hub ^of <f1> ^is <h1> ^output? <> yes ^mom <m>)
  -->
  (make sub-judice <h1>))


;;;IF   the rightmost child of a node has just been output,
;;;THEN   declare the node output
(p move::up:#
  (adjacent ^to <f> ^is # ^mom <m>)
  (hub ^of <f> ^output? yes ^mom <m>)
  {(hub ^is <m> ^output? <> yes)                    <mother>}
  -->
  (modify <mother> ^output? yes))


;;;IF   the rightmost subnode has just been output,
;;;THEN   declare the supernode output.
(p move::up:%
  (adjacent ^to <f> ^is % ^mom <m>)
  (hub ^of <f> ^output? yes ^super <super> ^mom <m>)
  {(hub ^is <super> ^output? <> yes)                <supernode>}
  -->
  (modify <supernode> ^output? yes))
```

Finally, there are the two LISP operators, GOAL and ASSERT (see Patten, 1986, §D.4), mentioned earlier. Unlike PRESELECT, which was written in LISP by necessity, GOAL and ASSERT have been written in LISP for reasons of efficiency. Almost every grammar production calls one of these two operators, so they greatly affect the efficiency of the system. (call GOAL feature <mom>) and (call ASSERT chosen feature <mom>) are equivalent to (make goal feature <mom>) and (make chosen feature <mom>) respectively, except that in each case the external routines check to make sure that feature has not already been chosen. This turns out to be faster than putting a –(chosen feature <mom>) condition in every grammar production.

The reason these external routines are so fast is that they take advantage of the hashing mechanism used by OPS5. Working memory elements are hashed on their first field. The elements that have the form (chosen ...) are stored in a list separate from the rest of working memory. A quick look at the source code of OPS5 reveals that this list can be retrieved by (get 'chosen 'wmpart*). Thus the feature check can be made by scanning a fraction of working memory.

6.4. Limitations of the current implementation

Some limitations of SLANG-I resulted from shortcuts taken to reduce the development time, complexity, and running time of the system. For instance, no checks are made to make sure exactly one feature is chosen from a system whose entry conditions are satisfied. No checks are made that preselected features actually exist. It is assumed that the networks form a coherent whole and that the input to the system will be reasonable. These checks would be easy to implement, but were excluded for reasons of simplicity and execution speed.

Several other limitations are the result of one major shortcut, viz. that what is essentially the OPS5 inference engine has been used as the "problem solver." Ideally a more sophisticated problem solver would perform forward- and backward-chaining. It would also have built-in mechanisms to handle disjunctive conditions (e.g. least commitment—see Stefik et al., 1983b, pp. 106-10) and would eliminate the need for GOAL and ASSERT. The results would be the same, but the mechanism would be less *ad hoc*.

6.5. Alternative implementations

There is no doubt that SLANG-I's straight OPS5 production rule implementation was only one of many possibilities. This section will suggest that other production systems and even object-oriented languages could, and perhaps should, be used in future implementations.

6.5.1. Other production systems

The advantages of essentially using the actual OPS5 mechanism as the problem solver for this initial implementation were its simplicity and speed. In practice, however, SLANG will be implemented within an expert system where the problem solving is done by a much more sophisticated inference engine. This problem solver may, for instance, have the ability to reason about the RHS of the production rules instead of simply trying to match the LHS. This may, for instance, enable the problem solver to "reason from first principles" by reasoning with the functional relationships described in the realization rules at the grammatical stratum in cases where no suitable compiled knowledge is available.

The point is that even with a representation almost identical to that used in SLANG-I, problem-solving techniques that are much more sophisticated than those built into OPS5 can be applied to text generation by a more sophisticated problem solver.

It must be considered, however, that speed will always be an important issue in practical text-generation work. Lengthy reasoning about language can only be tolerated in *some* rare circumstances. Thus, even though reasoning from first principles, as one example, is necessary to round-out SLANG's capabilities, the high-speed compiled approach demonstrated by SLANG-I must remain the dominant form of reasoning.

If a production system is used to implement SLANG then, it must have the ability to do simple forward- and backward-chaining very quickly. It should also have the flexibility to allow access to all parts of the production (including the effects) and efficiently implement backtracking and the techniques to avoid it (e.g. least commitment, Stefik et al., 1983b, pp. 106-10).

6.5.2. Inheritance hierarchies

One interesting possibility is that of representing system networks as inheritance hierarchies. This could be done, for instance, using a semantic network notation, or an object-oriented notation. Clauses, for instance, could be represented as a class of objects, finite clauses as a subclass of these, indicative clauses as a subclass of these, declarative clauses as a subclass of these and so on (note the use of of the term "class" corresponds exactly to the systemic term—see §3.3.1). Declarative clauses thus inherit the properties (represented by realization rules) of indicative clauses, finite clauses and clauses. In a sense, the backward-chaining of SLANG-I implements the mechanism of inheritance, but it may be more elegant and efficient if the problem solver performs inheritance as a primitive task. Of course the complex relationships found in system networks (including multiple inheritance) must be able to be represented in whatever notation is chosen. It may be that a hybrid representation (where, for instance, an inheritance hierarchy represents the systems and productions represent the gates) is best.

Indeed, returning to the fundamental relationship described in Chapter 4, SLANG should be able to be implemented using many of the tools and techniques developed to "construct [a] solution selectively and efficiently from a space of alternatives" (Hayes-Roth et al., 1983).

6.6. Summary

This chapter has discussed some of the implementation issues of SLANG and the implementation of a prototype system. This implementation uses an OPS5 representation for the system networks. The networks are translated from a LISP-based system network notation into the OPS5 productions. Gates are translated into forward-chaining productions, and other features are translated into backward-chaining productions. The realization rules, which appear as effects in the productions, are put in working memory as they are encountered in the form of OPS5 realization statements. Other productions, which are not part of the grammar but were written in OPS5 for convenience, then interpret these realization statements and build the linguistic structure of the text. Still other OPS5 productions perform the low-level behind-the-scenes work including writing out the text as it is generated.

Several shortcuts have been taken to reduce the size and complexity of the initial implementation. These included the omission of error checks, and the use of a slight abstraction of the OPS5 inference engine as the "problem solver" instead of implementing something more substantial. Finally, a straight production system implementation is only one possibility. Other problem-solving representations, in particular inheritance hierarchies—perhaps in conjunction with production rules—may work as well or better.

7
Related work in text generation

This chapter will compare and contrast the text-generation method described in the previous chapters with other recent work in the field. This will not include the large body of research done recently on discourse planning, but only work concerned with realizing these plans. The most notable exclusion on these grounds is McKeown's TEXT (McKeown, 1982, 1983, 1985) which sets some discourse-related goals then does the actual text generation using unguided search and backtracking (see Appelt, 1983, p. 599).

A look at recent systems reveals that there are currently two general approaches to text generation: the "grammar-oriented" approach and the "goal-oriented" approach. Both of these will be outlined, including their major practitioners, and the advantages that are offered.

Next, the systems that try to combine these two approaches will be considered. It will be shown that SLANG successfully achieves this, capturing the advantages of both the grammar-oriented and goal-oriented approaches.

7.1. The grammar-oriented approach

Several of the major text-generation projects are "grammar-oriented." This term will be used to refer to those systems that traverse an explicit linguistic grammar. Since the flow of control is directed by the grammar traversal, the logical structure of the system reflects the structure of the grammar.

The original grammar-oriented systems would simply traverse the grammar, typically an ATN, backtracking where necessary. More recent grammar-oriented systems avoid backing up by doing an analysis at choice points to make sure the right decision is made the first time. This analysis often involves considering semantic and pragmatic issues that, for reasons of modularity, should not be directly accessible to the grammar. Therefore an interface mechanism of some kind is provided through which the higher-level guidance may be obtained. Two grammar-oriented systems will now be surveyed.

7.1.1. PROTEUS

PROTEUS (Davey, 1978) is a program for annotating games of noughts and crosses (tic-tac-toe). It produces fluent text in this limited domain, with particular emphasis on referring expressions and ellipsis. PROTEUS traverses an explicit systemic grammar in order of delicacy (from left to right). Some features will already have been chosen when the grammar is entered, but most decisions at choice points are made by "specialists." Some specialists consider the text that has been produced so far, and the "semantic specialists" consult the non-linguistic domain knowledge for guidance. The program either plays a game itself or accepts the moves of a game as input. In either case the game annotation begins with a transcript of a valid set of moves.

An example from Davey (1978, p. 17):

The following commentary was given on the moves shown:

'The game began with my taking a corner,
and you took an adjacent one.

P		A

I threatened you by taking the corner
adjacent to the one that you had just
taken, but you blocked my diagonal
and threatened me.

		P
	A	
P		A

I blocked yours and forked you.

P		P
	A	
P		A

Although you blocked one of my edges
and threatened me, I won by completing
the other.'

P	P	P
A	A	
P		A

The general procedure is to choose some number of consecutive moves to be described in a sentence, to generate this, and to repeat. First the tactical significance of the moves is determined. Then, depending on this, descriptions of the appropriate moves are conjoined to form a sentence of not more than three main clauses.

The actual sentences are formed by traversing system networks. When faced with a choice, PROTEUS calls upon a "specialist procedure" to make a decision based on the "syntactic and semantic context." These specialists may actually generate bits of text as part of the decision process to see, for instance, if a satisfactory modifier or qualifier can be constructed. Davey claims that

> It will therefore be obvious that the program's operations cannot be categorized as working 'top-down'. It does not invariably construct an item by determining its feature-set, thence determining constituent-structure, and finally building each constituent. Instead, syntax and semantics are woven together and dependent on each other, either one being able to take control as the situation demands. (ibid., pp. 120-1).

When traversing the network, PROTEUS uses defaults to save some work. For instance, unless told otherwise it assumes clauses are *independent, indicative, declarative,* and *past.* This would not be useful except in the restricted register in which PROTEUS operates.

One interesting aspect of the semantic specialists is that they may choose several features at a time as opposed to the "one feature, one specialist" approach adopted in Nigel (see below). For example, if a semantic specialist decides a relative clause is necessary, it preselects (not a term used by Davey) *clause, dependent, finite,* and *relative.* The semantic specialists may also decide that a special time adverb or aspect is required, and again it will preselect the necessary clause features.

PROTEUS has similar specialists to help construct referring expressions. These can be quite complex: "the corner common to the edge opposite the square X had just taken and the one opposite the square O had just taken" (ibid., p. 144).

In summary, PROTEUS produced impressive results in the limited domain but relied on *ad hoc* procedures and "specialists" to a large degree. Despite the shortcomings of the implementation, PROTEUS became a major influence in text-generation research since essentially the same approach was adopted for the Nigel system.

7.1.2. Nigel

Nigel (Mann et al., 1983; Mann, 1985) is a general purpose text-generation system very similar in design to PROTEUS. It too is built around an explicit systemic grammar, and the grammar itself has been the focus of most of the work. As in PROTEUS, the grammar is traversed in order of delicacy, from left to right. The decisions at choice points (systems) are handled by "choosers," that are organized and documented much better than Davey's specialists. These "choosers," like Davey's specialists, are not part of the linguistic theory, and act as a special interface through which semantic/pragmatic considerations can be brought to bear on choices in the grammar. The relevant semantic/pragmatic considerations are collectively termed the "environment." The "environment" knows about the text plan and goals of the speaker, and has access to the non-linguistic domain knowledge. The choosers base their decision on the answers received in response to specific questions posed to the "environment."

As an example of how the grammar is traversed, consider the informal description of how the mood of a clause is chosen (Mann et al., 1983, p. 41). The grammar finds itself in a system where the choice is between *indicative* and *imperative*. The chooser asks the environment, "Is the illocutionary point of the surface level speech act ... a command, i.e. a request of an action by the hearer?" The environment then answers, "It's not intended to command." So the chooser chooses *indicative*. The grammar, having just passed through one system, now finds itself at another labelled "IndicativeType" where the choice is between *declarative* and *interrogative*. The chooser for this system asks the environment, "Is the illocutionary point of the surface level speech act ... to state?" And the environment answers, "Yes, it's intended to state." The chooser therefore chooses *declarative*. Any realization rules attached to the features are processed as soon as they are chosen. This same "question and answer" procedure is repeated for every system encountered during the traversal.[5] The clause network is traversed again for any embedded clauses, the nominal-group network is traversed for any nominal groups required and so on. Nigel will be discussed further in §7.4 below.

7.1.3. Advantages of grammar-oriented systems

The grammar-oriented approach, of which PROTEUS and Nigel are examples, has several important advantages. The grammars may be represented in a linguistic formalism since no processing information needs to be included. This is advantageous because it means that grammar can be judged, modified, understood etc., independently of the rest of the system (Appelt, 1982). In addition, the logical structure of the system is explicit in the grammar. This makes the operation of the system easier to understand.

In general, these advantages are conducive to research projects, like PRO-TEUS and Nigel, that are primarily concerned with linguistic issues rather than with processing.

7.2. The goal-oriented approach

On the other side of the text-generation coin are systems that generate text by goal-directed problem solving. The control in these systems typically rests with some form of text planner; the flow of control is driven by the goals the planner is trying to achieve. It is the *mechanism* of this planner and the interface with the grammatical component which is of interest in these systems. The grammar itself is often relegated to an obscure if not invisible role. They tend to regard the form of the linguistic component (LC) as being subsidiary to, or even dependent on, the goal-directed problem solving.

> [W]e believe (and it is here that we part company with researchers such as Mann and Matthiessen [1983] whose aims we otherwise share) that the demands placed on the LC by the need to work efficiently from a plan have overriding implications for the LC's architecture. (McDonald et al., 1985, p. 800)

This is not intended to imply that grammar-oriented systems are incompatible with such goals—but merely that grammar-oriented systems are prepared to make sacrifices in clarity and efficiency of goal processing toward linguistic integrity of the grammar, while goal-oriented systems are willing to make linguistic sacrifices toward the goal-directed processing. Consider the choosers in Nigel. The choices that are made often depend on consideration of the goals of the speaker as represented in the environment (Mann et al., 1983). Clearly in some sense Nigel is therefore *directed* by these goals, but the choosers are invoked in the first place because of their position in the grammar, not because a particular goal emerged.

Two examples of goal-oriented text generators are Appelt's KAMP and the work involving McDonald's MUMBLE.

7.2.1. KAMP

KAMP (Appelt, 1982) is a planner that integrates linguistic and other types of actions to achieve communicative goals. The important issues in KAMP are this integration, and the ability to reason about the knowledge and intentions of

137

other discourse participants.

Consider a situation (from ibid., p. 2) where there are two agents, A and B, working in a shop where there are several objects on a table. Suppose agent A knows agent B wants to perform a particular task. Suppose agent A wants to help agent B by telling him to use a particular tool with which agent B is unfamiliar. Agent A may, for instance, point to one of the objects and say "Use the wheel-puller to remove the flywheel." In this case the speaker has combined a non-linguistic act (pointing) and a linguistic act to achieve two goals: first to communicate which tool to use, and second to communicate the name of the tool for future use.

Suppose further that, in a similar situation, the speaker had his hands full and there was no satisfactory verbal description of the wheel-puller. The speaker would then have to plan to put down what he was carrying and again point to the tool while giving his advice. Thus there is a potential for complex interactions between linguistic and non-linguistic acts that are integrated. These interactions can be resolved, however, by an AI problem solver. KAMP is the problem solver Appelt constructed to explore and illustrate these ideas.

In the last example it was important that the speaker knew that the hearer didn't know the name of the necessary tool—otherwise the pointing action is redundant. Similarly, the entire episode would have been unnecessary if agent A had known that agent B already knew what tool to use. It is clear that in communication of this sort, reasoning about the knowledge of the agents involved is required. Appelt illustrates this kind of reasoning with an example (ibid., p.83):

Consider the following problem:

A robot named Rob and a man named John are in a room that is adjacent to a hallway containing a calendar. Both Rob and John are capable of moving, reading calendars, and talking to each other, and they each know that everyone is capable of performing these actions. They both know they are in the room, and they both know where the hallway is. Neither Rob nor John knows what date it is. Suppose further that John wants to know what day it is, and Rob knows he does. Furthermore, Rob is helpful and wants to do what he can to ensure that John achieves his goal. We would like to see KAMP devise a plan, perhaps involving actions by both Rob and John, that will result in John knowing what day it is.

We would like to see Rob devise a plan that consists of a choice between two alternatives. First, if John could find out where the calendar is, he could go to the calendar and read it, and in the resulting state would know the date. So, Rob might tell John where the calendar is, reasoning that this information is sufficient for John to form and execute a plan that would achieve his goal. The second alternative is for Rob to move into the hall and read the calendar himself, move back into the room, and tell John the date.

KAMP solves the problem by doing hierarchical planning (Sacerdoti, 1975) with predicates and instantiations such as KnowsWhatIs(Rob, date), and actions such as Do(Rob, Move(loc(Rob), Loc(cal1))) and Do(Rob, Inform(John, Date=D)).

Thus KAMP can solve this type of problem by goal-directed reasoning about the mental states of agents including itself, and about the interactions between the linguistic and non-linguistic acts involved. But unfortunately, the grammar is built into the planner *ad hoc* and is thus not easily accessible or observable (Appelt, 1983).

7.2.2. MUMBLE

The other major goal-oriented work is that of McDonald (1980, 1983a, 1983b and McDonald et al., 1985). This, like KAMP, is primarily concerned with the achievement of goals and the organization of language generation, not grammatical issues.

McDonald labels his control structure as "description directed control." The description is of the final text, but at a very high level of abstraction. This description can be regarded as a special notation for specifying sets of goals.

The general organization of McDonald's most recent work (McDonald et al., 1985) is that of a pipeline performing four operations concurrently. The first step is "planning," using specific script-like knowledge for specific linguistic registers. In the example domain, legal discourse, these scripts are "Describe-legal-case," "Describe-a-party-to-a-case," "Describe-corporate-party," etc. Additional register information is included in the plan labelled as "perspectives," such as "establish-relation-of-speaker," and "misappropriation-script."

The second step is "attachment." The parts of the plan are attached to a phrase-structure representation according to various grammatical constraints and some "stylistic rules" indicating the preferred length and complexity of sentences for a particular register.

The third step in the pipeline is "realization." Here the high-level representation attached to the phrase-structure tree is realized as a phrase-structure sub-tree. The process annotates the nodes with functional labels and morphological information to help constrain further processing.

The fourth step in the pipeline is the "phrase-structure execution." At this step the phrase-structure representation built by the last step is traversed, recursively traversing subtrees and outputting lexical items attached to leaf nodes.

The interest here is in *what* information gets passed *when* between the various components. The grammar in MUMBLE, like that of KAMP, is built into the workings of the program and is not presented as being a major issue.

7.2.3. Advantages of the goal-oriented approach

The goal-oriented approach also has some important advantages. One particularly important characteristic of the goal-oriented systems is that there is no full grammar traversal. The grammatical processing is restricted to responding directly to specific goals, and therefore may be more selective and efficient.

The goal-oriented approach also allows linguistic and non-linguistic acts to be integrated in a coherent framework. This important type of reasoning is obscured somewhat by a strictly grammar-oriented approach.

More abstractly, the goal-oriented approach seems to be more consistent with the aims of the computational paradigm (as described by Winograd, 1983, p. 21) than the grammar-oriented approach. This is not surprising since the emphasis in this paradigm is on processing. The computational paradigm tries to apply general problem-solving techniques to processing language. One of the most powerful problem-solving techniques is goal-directed search (see §2.2.4) which, applied to language generation, is the goal-oriented approach.

7.3. Combining the approaches

Both the grammar-oriented and goal-oriented approaches have advantages. Ideally the explicit grammar and logical structure of the grammar-oriented approach could be combined with the efficient goal-oriented problem-solving approach.

7.3.1. TELEGRAM

TELEGRAM (Appelt, 1983) was an attempt to combine KAMP's emphasis on planning throughout the generation with an explicit grammar (in this case a functional unification grammar). Although TELEGRAM had a planner *available* throughout the generation, the primary locus of control was in the grammar.

> [T]he TELEGRAM planner will create a high-level functional description of the intended utterance. ... At this point, the planner is no longer directly in control of the planning process. The planner invokes the unifier with the above text functional description, and the grammar functional description, and relinquishes control to the unification process.

> The unification process follows the [unification algorithm] until there is either an alternative in the grammar that needs to be selected, or some feature in the text FD does not unify with any feature in the grammar FD. (Appelt, 1983, p. 598)

For cases where the unification does in fact fail, the grammar is "annotated" with special signals to tell the unifier to invoke the planner with certain goals. Suppose the unifier is trying to unify a functional description for an NP with the corresponding part of the grammar. Suppose that the unification will not be successful because there is no *referent* feature in the textual functional description to unify with the grammar (ibid., p. 598). The *referent* feature, however, may have an annotation that tells the unifier to invoke the planner to plan the referent. The planner will reason, as KAMP did, about the knowledge of the discourse participants and work toward a functional description suitable for the unification at hand. If no suitable plans can be found using linguistic acts, the planner can insert non-linguistic acts (e.g. pointing) into the plan as KAMP did.

Although descriptions of TELEGRAM place heavy emphasis on the role of the planner, it really has the design of a grammar-oriented system similar to Nigel: "the system 'choosers' of Nigel play a role similar to the annotation on the alternatives in TELEGRAM, and many other parallels can be drawn" (ibid., p. 599). Thus, like Nigel, TELEGRAM needs a special interface (the annotations) through which semantic/pragmatic criteria can guide the traversal. This guidance is critical since unification alone amounts to a blind search.

> In spite of its advantages, there are some serious problems with unification grammar if it is employed straightforwardly in a language planning system. One of the most serious problems is the inefficiency of the unification algorithm ... A straightforward application of that algorithm is very expensive, consuming an order-of-magnitude more time in the unification process than in the entire planning process leading up to the construction of the text FD. The problem is not simply one of efficiency of implementation. It is inherent in any algorithm that searches alternatives blindly and thereby does work that is exponentially related to the number of alternatives in the grammar. Any solution to the problem must be a conceptual one that minimizes the number of alternatives that ever have to be considered. (Ibid., p. 596).

Although TELEGRAM's planner reduces this problem, the unification process is still in control, and in common with Nigel this prevents other problem-solving techniques (like backward-chaining) to be used to reduce even further the number of alternatives considered. Whenever a choice is encountered by the unifier, the problem solver is invoked to make a decision based on the "annotations" attached to the various choices. The point is that the annotations of all the choices have to be considered explicitly.

In summary, TELEGRAM achieves the advantages of a grammar-oriented system while maintaining KAMP's ability to integrate linguistic and non-linguistic actions. However, two of the advantages of goal-oriented systems have still been sacrificed: a special interface is required, and the computational efficiency of having the problem solver in control has been lost.

7.3.2. SLANG

As TELEGRAM demonstrated, the difficulty in achieving the advantages of both the grammar-oriented and goal-oriented approaches lies in interfacing the goal-directed problem solver with a linguistically formalized grammar. The SLANG system does not have this problem because of the conflation described in Chapter 4.

SLANG's grammar, even though it is represented in a linguistic formalism, can be interpreted as problem-solving knowledge by a goal-directed problem solver. The key phenomenon here is that the control dictated by the goals and the control dictated by the grammar are the same—they have been conflated. This makes SLANG both a grammar-oriented *and* a goal-oriented method.

First, consider that the conflation of grammar and knowledge base in SLANG gives it the desirable characteristics of the grammar-oriented systems. Specifically, this means that the grammar can be judged, modified etc. independently of the rest of the system. The logical structure is also explicit in the structure of the grammar, making the method comparatively easy to visualize and understand.

Despite the fact that the grammar is processed in the opposite direction to PROTEUS and Nigel, SLANG is still a grammar-oriented method. An explicit grammar is still followed and provides the logical structure of the grammatical processing—the difference is that features in SLANG are *also* interpreted as goals, so the grammar can be processed by efficient goal-directed techniques.

The conflation of grammar and knowledge base also means that SLANG is a goal-oriented system and thus inherits the desirable characteristics of that approach. The control structure is goal-directed backward-chaining starting from communicative goals (semantic features). For instance, since SLANG's activities are initiated and governed by a general-purpose problem solver, and general-purpose problem solving can be conflated with behavioural potential (see §4.2.6), SLANG provides a suitable framework for the integration of linguistic and non-linguistic acts—although this line of research has not been pursued.

Finally, SLANG inherits the advantage of being able to apply powerful AI techniques to the generation, with all the computational and theoretical benefits this implies, instead of relying on a special *ad hoc* component.

7.4. Problem reduction in Nigel and SLANG

For the purpose of clearly illustrating the grammar-oriented nature of Nigel, the above discussion (§7.1.2) provided only a brief overview of that system's characteristics. Since, however, it is the best-known systemic text-generation system, a more detailed examination of Nigel—and its relation to the SLANG system—is called for at this point.

The most obvious difference between Nigel and SLANG is that the former processes the grammar from left to right, starting at the least delicate features and working through increasingly delicate systems; while the latter processes the grammar from right to left, starting at the most delicate systems and working through decreasingly delicate systems. This is, of course, in itself not a significant difference between the two systems. Furthermore, gates are processed identically, and for cases where features are preselected by realization rules at the grammatical stratum (e.g. a nominal-group feature preselected from the clause network), Nigel has a procedure called "path augmentation" that seems similar to SLANG's backward-chaining.

> Any feature in the system network has one or more *paths* leading to it, i.e., a set of choices through which it can be reached. As long as there is only one path leading to the feature, it can be preselected, and its path computed through redundancy, so-called *path augmentation*. In other words, on a unique path only the most delicate feature need be preselected. (Mann et al., 1983, p. 68)

The key distinction between Nigel and SLANG is therefore the interface between the semantics and the grammar, and the processing directly affected by the interface. That is, the key distinction is SLANG's interface by preselection of seed features as opposed to Nigel's interface using choosers. The significant difference is that once the compiled knowledge in the semantic stratum preselects the seed features in SLANG, all other grammatical features are determined—there are no further decisions that must be made explicitly; whereas Nigel's choosers must make many explicit decisions before the most delicate systems, and it must also make explicit decisions regarding those features that would be preselected in SLANG. The point is that SLANG, unlike Nigel, is never required to explicitly choose between *finite* and *non-finite*, between *imperative* and *indicative,* between *declarative* and *interrogative* and so on, because these choices are determined by the choice of more delicate features. SLANG gains this advantage because it exploits the knowledge in the semantic stratum (as described by Halliday, 1978), that links specific social registers to specific grammatical features.

Another problem Nigel faces as a result of the chooser approach is the problem of coordinating the decisions made by the different choosers—which may be interdependent. When the traversal reaches the system to choose the number of an indicative Subject, the chooser asks the environment, "Is the [Subject] inherently multiple, i.e., a set or collection of things, or unitary?" (Mann et al., 1983). The problem is that at this point in the traversal, the Subject may not yet be conflated with another function for which this information is available. In that case the environment cannot answer the question. Mann suggests that it would be unreasonable to suspend the decision until later because the entire system might eventually get stalled. He therefore suggests that the grammar could be rewritten so that the choices are guaranteed to be made only when the information is known at that point in the traversal (Mann, 1985). It seems unreasonable, however, to place restrictions on the grammar to suit Nigel's computational characteristics—clearly this defeats the purpose of using a linguistic grammar. Note that SLANG does not suffer from this problem since all explicit choices are made before the grammar is processed.

It is interesting to note that both Nigel and SLANG can be viewed as using the problem-solving strategy of problem reduction (see Nilsson, 1971, pp. 80-123; and §5.8). Nigel can be viewed as having a problem-reduction methodology where the start nodes of the AND/OR graphs are the root features of the system networks. So the "initial problem" to construct a *clause,* for instance, is reduced to making it either *finite* OR *non-finite,* AND making it either *material-process, mental-process, verbal-process* OR *relational-process,* and so on. The problem of making it *finite* is reduced to making it either *indicative* OR *imperative* and so on through the entire system network.

The problem that Nigel faces is that most of the reductions are to OR nodes, since in this formulation any feature that is a term in a system will be represented by an OR node. Thus the problem solver does not know which of the OR nodes should be reduced. The choosers make these decisions after interacting with the environment.

In SLANG, the start nodes are seed features and the AND/OR graphs stretch from them back to the root features. The result of this, the preselection of independent disjuncts, and being able to treat dependent disjuncts as solved, is that there are no OR nodes in SLANG's AND/OR graph. This means that once the initial goals have been set, SLANG can proceed deterministically with no need for interaction with other components and only considering those nodes that will be in the solution graph (see §5.8). The compiled knowledge in the semantic stratum allows SLANG to set seed features as initial problems and do problem reduction against the grain of the systems, avoiding the disjunction.

SLANG and Nigel produce the same result, and the same implicit grammatical choices are made by the two methods (i.e. the grammatical search space is the same), but the compiled knowledge in the semantic stratum and the goal-oriented processing make SLANG's search more selective and more efficient.

A question which could be asked at this point is: "Intuitively speaking, if both Nigel and SLANG are doing problem reduction, why is there such a difference?" The answer is that the goals in Nigel's case (the start nodes) are vacuous—saying that the solution must be a clause conveys almost no information to the problem solver. The goals SLANG works from, *unmarked-declarative-theme, addressee-subject* and so on, provide enough information for the problem solver to find the solution selectively without recourse to outside help. This is a result of the compiled knowledge contained in the semantic stratum exploited by SLANG—the strictly grammar-oriented nature of Nigel prevents the grammar traversal from being compiled out.

7.5. Summary

This chapter has briefly reviewed the two major approaches to text generation, the grammar-oriented approach and the goal-oriented approach, and shown that SLANG in fact fits *both* descriptions.

The grammar-oriented approach has the advantages of using an explicit grammar represented in a linguistic formalism. Since this grammar is simply traversed, the control structure of the system is explicit. The goal-oriented approach has the main advantage of directly applying powerful AI techniques throughout the generation for efficient and selective processing.

The difficulty of interfacing a goal-directed problem solver with a linguistic grammar is overcome by the conflation of grammar and knowledge base. As a result, SLANG benefits from the advantages of both the grammar-oriented and goal-oriented approaches to text generation.

8
Conclusions

This final chapter consists of four parts. First, the main points from the previous chapters will be summarized, giving a condensed description of the work done on the SLANG approach to text generation. Second, the problems that may impede progress on SLANG will be examined. Third, some ideas for future research will be explored. Fourth, the concluding remarks will include an evaluation of SLANG and the current progress, and the prospects for the future.

8.1. Summary

8.1.1. The problem

One problem that has persistently occupied and bedevilled text-generation research is how to interface higher-level reasoning with an explicit grammar written in an established linguistic formalism. This problem is central to text generation because of the computational and linguistic requirements of the task.

Text generation involves an enormous, complex search space, yet must be performed quickly if it is to be effective. These characteristics suggest that text generation requires the powerful knowledge-based computational methods—such as forward-chaining and goal-directed backward-chaining—developed in AI over the past fifteen years.

Text generation also has important linguistic requirements. Specifically, an explicit grammar that is represented in an established linguistic formalism is required. This enables direct input from linguists and the linguistic literature. It also allows the grammar to be understood, judged, modified and so on, independently of the computational concerns (Appelt, 1982). Finally, assuming that the

146

processing is guided by the explicit grammar, the grammar can provide a useful display of the logical structure of the text-generation process.

The problem of interfacing the AI problem-solving techniques with the linguistic formalism arises because of the apparent incompatibility of the representations involved. The computational representations on the one hand have been developed with issues such as selectivity and efficiency in mind. The linguistic representations on the other hand have been developed for the purpose of perspicuously describing particular areas of linguistic theory.

8.1.2. The solution

The solution to the problem of interfacing AI problem-solving techniques and an established linguistic formalism has involved identifying a linguistic formalism that in fact uses the same representation as the required problem-solving methods. Ironically, this linguistic formalism originated not from mathematics or from the theory of computation, but from anthropology. The formalism is Halliday's systemic grammar, which originated from the work of the anthropologist Malinowski and the sociolinguist Firth.

The shared representation, which is the basis of this solution, resulted from the historical accident that at the core of both AI problem solving and systemic grammar is the representation of a space of alternatives. In each case this representation consists of describing the conditions under which an alternative is appropriate, and the effects or consequences of that alternative. Systemic grammar is probably unique in having this fundamental relationship with AI problem solving because the emphasis on paradigmatic description is an invention of Halliday.

The common representation means that in fact *no* interface *per se* is needed at all. An AI problem solver can simply interpret a systemic grammar as linguistic knowledge to be used to solve linguistic problems, in exactly the same way as it can use chemistry to solve chemistry problems, or medical knowledge to solve medical problems. Indeed, it is only because there is no interface *per se* that the solution is possible—otherwise the powerful computational techniques embodied in the problem solver would lose control to the interface component during the processing of the grammar.

A significant advantage of SLANG is that it embodies linguistically, and exploits computationally, Halliday's semantic stratum of systemic theory. Computationally, the semantic stratum acts as a body of large-grain-size compiled knowledge that guides the problem solving at the grammatical stratum. Thus the semantic stratum serves linguistically to link the grammar to the social situation, and computationally to increase significantly the speed of the text generation.

The resulting approach to text generation, then, uses the state-of-the-art computational techniques (e.g. forward-chaining, goal-directed backward-chaining, and knowledge compilation), and an explicit grammar—including the semantics—represented in an established linguistic formalism.

8.1.3. The formal model

One of the interesting results of the fundamental relationship between AI problem solving and systemic grammar is the formal model presented in Chapter 5. Systemic grammar has always lacked the formal treatment available for grammars of mathematical origin. However, since the common representation allows a systemic grammar to be interpreted as a set of productions (a common AI representation), an almost traditional formalization in terms of productions can be given.

A formal treatment of the SLANG model can then be given in terms of the formalized grammar and formal algorithms from the AI literature (in particular, problem reduction). Results can then be proven concerning issues such as completeness and soundness. This formal model of systemic grammar demonstrates that systemic grammar can be rigorously formalized in terms of rules, without compromising the functional description.

8.1.4. The implementation

For the purposes of testing and demonstrating SLANG, a prototype system was constructed using a grammar pieced together from several sources. Several shortcuts were taken to keep the project manageable: the phonological/orthographic stratum, the clause-complex rank and the morphological rank were omitted, the word rank is small and *ad hoc,* and only a very small semantic stratum has been implemented. Nevertheless, the system adequately shows the processing of a large system network (the clause systems), interstratal preselection, and inter-rank preselection. The system was tested by generating examples (see Appendix B) from several domains.

The test system, SLANG-I, is written in the production language OPS5. The systemic grammar is stored as a set of OPS5 productions after being translated from a LISP-based system network notation. The grammar can then be loaded into OPS5 and used directly to to do forward- and backward-chaining. The text-generation system itself is very simple, consisting of a small number of productions and LISP operators to build linguistic structures from realization rules and to do low-level maintenance.

8.1.5. Related work in text generation

Finally, a comparison was made between SLANG and some related text-generation projects. It was observed that all the projects could be classified as either grammar-oriented, goal-oriented, or an attempt to combine the two. Grammar-oriented systems have two main advantages: the grammars can be understood, judged, and modified independently of the computational aspects of the system; and the grammar provides an explicit and useful display of the logical structure of the text-generation process. Goal-oriented systems have the main advantage of exploiting powerful goal-directed AI problem-solving techniques to efficiently and selectively generate text.

Davey's PROTEUS and Mann's Nigel are clearly grammar-oriented systems, Appelt's KAMP and McDonald's MUMBLE are clearly goal-oriented systems, while Appelt's TELEGRAM and SLANG are attempts to combine the grammar-oriented and goal-oriented approaches to achieve the advantages of both.

Although TELEGRAM was an attempt to combine the grammar-oriented and goal-oriented approaches, it fell short of this aim because of the problem of interfacing the AI problem-solving methods with the functional unification formalism. The systemic grammar in SLANG, on the contrary, can be used directly as

149

linguistic problem-solving knowledge by a state-of-the-art AI problem solver. Thus SLANG is able to achieve successfully the advantages of both the grammar-oriented and goal-oriented approaches.

8.2. Major problems

Though the preceding arguments have hopefully convinced the reader that SLANG represents a promising new approach to text generation, there are still some problems to be overcome before this promise can be fully realized. These problems are not computational—given only the existing computational methodologies, and existing hardware and software tools, SLANG should be able to provide an effective, practical text-generation facility, given sufficient linguistic resources. The problem is that sufficient linguistic resources do not yet exist.

The relatively small number of linguists working within the systemic framework has severely restricted the availability and coverage of the grammars. Only small subsets of English are covered, even for areas that have received the most attention (e.g. the clause). Large components of the grammatical description have been left untouched (for instance, it seems no substantial work has been done on the systemic morphology of English). Often the level of detail of grammars in the linguistic literature is not suitable for computational treatment.

The grammar developed by Mann et al. (1983) and the grammar pieced together for SLANG-I indicate that at least for the grammatical stratum, the large system networks necessary for practical text generation *can* be constructed. The doubt really lies with the semantic stratum. But even here, one of the most difficult issues—the organization—has already been resolved. The semantic stratum is a paradigmatic description of register, as prescribed by Halliday (1978).

The obvious application for SLANG is text generation in expert systems. Some linguistic work on particular expert-system domains has been done within the systemic framework (e.g. Mishler, 1984), but unfortunately no sufficiently detailed semantic analyses of expert-system domains are currently available. Nevertheless, several considerations in the field of expert systems justify an optimistic outlook on the semantic stratum.

Expert systems—almost by definition—work in very restricted domains (see Brachman et al., 1983, p. 42). In many cases at least, this implies that the linguistic registers involved will also be very restricted. The high degree of specialization that makes the non-linguistic domain knowledge manageable yet practical, may also make the semantic knowledge manageable yet practical.

Another point is that the semantic stratum could potentially be developed to a large extent during the normal knowledge-acquisition-engineering process when building an expert system. Note that linguistic observation is already part of the recommended procedure:

> In addition, the knowledge engineer also listens for justifications of the associations, terms, and strategical methods the expert uses when solving a problem. These are important to record not only for the knowledge engineer's own clarification but also for maintaining adequate system documentation and allowing accurate system explanations. (Buchanan et al., 1983, p.135)

> The knowledge engineer schedules numerous meetings with the expert over a period of a few months to uncover the basic concepts, primitive relations, and definitions needed to talk about the problem and its solutions. (ibid., p. 133)

> *Record a detailed protocol of the expert solving at least one prototypical case.*
> ... It provides a list of vocabulary terms and hints about strategies. (ibid., p. 161)

In addition to a study of the terms the expert uses in particular registers, the grammatical constructions used in those registers could also be noted.

No doubt the construction of semantic strata will be slow and painful in the beginning. But, as more experience accumulates, and generalizations are passed on, and techniques are developed, building a semantic stratum may become no worse than any other area of knowledge acquisition and engineering.

8.3. Future research

Given the exploratory nature of this work, it is not surprising that there are several interesting continuations and offshoot ideas that can be pursued in future research. Two obvious continuations—the incorporation of SLANG into a full-scale expert system, and the improvement of the currently implemented linguistic capabilities—will be touched on first. Then a technical offshoot concerning highly-compiled semantics will be looked at. Finally, the possibility and implications of the SLANG ideas for parsing will be explored.

8.3.1. Incorporation of SLANG into an expert system
One obvious continuation of the present work is to incorporate SLANG as the text-generation component of an expert system. This would allow SLANG to be studied in the context of a full-blown AI problem solver, and would provide an opportunity to examine the requirements of the semantic stratum objectively.

8.3.2. Supplementary linguistic treatment
An interesting and practical extension to this work would be to implement the phonological stratum and use SLANG to do speech generation. Halliday already has a relatively well-developed treatment of phonology, especially intonation and rhythm, and its relation to the rest of the linguistic system (e.g. see Halliday, 1976d; and Halliday, 1985, Chapter 8). This would also involve augmenting the grammatical stratum. Specifically, another functional analysis would have to be included: the analysis of Given and New (see also Halliday, 1985, pp. 274-81 and Winograd, 1983, pp. 284-5) as part of the textual metafunction. Realization rules would have to be added to the grammatical stratum to preselect appropriate phonological features.

Although the grammatical stratum forms the bulk of the implementation, shortcuts have been taken in the current implementation. Both the top and bottom ranks have been omitted—neither the clause-complex nor the morphological rank has been implemented. The former has not been needed because the examples have been so small, and the latter has been avoided by greatly constraining the size of the dictionary and listing all morphological forms explicitly. It is clear, however, that in a larger system—even a larger prototype—both of these ranks would be absolutely necessary.

Another potentially useful idea is the *unmarked feature*. These appear often in the systemic literature, and are indicated by an asterisk (e.g. Figure 4.6). The idea is that if the entry conditions for a system are satisfied, and none of the other features have been chosen, then the unmarked feature is chosen by default. The usefulness of this particular mechanism is suggested by the interest in default reasoning in AI problem solving (e.g. Stefik et al., 1983a, p. 73). A set of productions, one for each default feature, could be introduced which have the entry conditions of the system as conditions and the choice of the features as the effect. Some mechanism would also have to be added to make sure all other avenues of reasoning are explored before any default production fires. It is not clear if the advantages of such default reasoning outweigh the added complexity.

8.3.3. Further compilation

The semantic stratum was described in Chapter 4 as "compiled knowledge" that guides the problem solving at the grammatical stratum. It was pointed out (§4.2.5) that the knowledge at the semantic stratum could potentially be compiled further by precomputing the inference at the grammatical stratum and attaching the results directly to the semantic features in the internal representation. For the purposes of discussion, this further compilation will be called "hypercompilation."

The process of hypercompilation would involve looking at each preselection statement at the semantic stratum, precomputing the resulting forward- and backward-chaining as far as possible (including following any preselection statements leading to lower ranks and strata), and collecting the realization rules attached to the features involved. The realization rules are then attached directly to the original semantic feature in place of the preselection rule. All this is done automatically, and is transparent to the grammar writer. This means that very sophisticated computational techniques can be used during the hypercompilation, including keeping detailed tables, carefully looking for redundant realization rules, and so on. If the linguist makes a change to the system networks at any stratum, the hypercompilation is done again, perhaps incrementally. It may be desirable for the computational linguist to designate only certain portions (e.g. high-frequency registers) of the semantic stratum for hypercompilation.

The idea of hypercompilation is very vague at this stage, but it may be worth investigating. It appears that it may allow a significant increase in the speed of the text generation, while being linguistically transparent.

8.3.4. Reasoning with knowledge at the grammatical stratum

Another topic related to knowledge compilation is the possibility of "reasoning from first principles" (see §2.3.3) with the knowledge at the grammatical stratum. It is possible that the grammatical stratum could be used as base-level knowledge to solve problems when there is no appropriate compiled knowledge available (insufficient semantic knowledge) or to provide automatic linguistic explanations of generated text, since the use of compiled knowledge prevents the automatic generation of teleological explanations.

One example of this kind of reasoning—solving the goal of conflating the Agent and the Theme—has already been described in detail (§4.2.4). It is unclear, however, how far this type of reasoning can be taken.

8.3.5. Natural-language understanding

The final point for future research is to investigate the implications of the present work for natural-language understanding. The major problem that has been solved here is how to interface AI problem solving with a linguistic formalism. It was shown how the higher levels of linguistic and non-linguistic knowledge could be used to process the grammar selectively and efficiently. The main point to be made in this section is that the same problem occurs in natural-language understanding, and that the same solution also may apply.

Parsing, like text generation, is a task that requires substantial guidance from higher-level knowledge. Parsing also preferably uses an established linguistic formalism. Thus the same interface problem that occurs in text generation also occurs in parsing. The solution to the problem in text generation may also work for parsing.

The semantic stratum, during a parse, can preselect features from the grammatical stratum. In this case the preselections represent hypotheses instead of goals, but the same forward- and backward-chaining can be done to determine all the implications of these hypotheses. The suggestion that the semantic stratum, representing knowledge of register, could be useful when parsing should not be surprising. As Halliday says, given a particular register

> ... we can predict quite a lot about the language that will be used, in respect of the meanings and the significant grammatical and lexical features through which they are expressed. If the entries under field, tenor and mode are filled out carefully and thoughtfully, it is surprising how many of the features of the language turn out to be relatable to the context of situation. This is not to claim that we know what the participants are going to say; it merely shows that we can make sensible and informed guesses about certain aspects of what they might say, with a reasonable probability of being right. There is always, in language, the freedom to act untypically—but that in itself serves to confirm the reality of the concept of what is typical. (Halliday, 1978, p. 226)

If the register could only be ascertained by linguistic means, then using knowledge of register to help understand language would be begging the question. This is not the case however. Register is largely determined from outside language. Field and tenor in particular, are determined, to a large extent, before any linguistic interaction occurs at all. The physical setting, the social status of the participants, and even the emotional issues at the moment (see §3.5), can often be ascertained easily without linguistic interaction.

> The linguistic system ... is organized in such a way that the social context is predictive of the text. This is what makes it possible for a member to make the necessary predictions about the meanings that are being exchanged in any situation which he encounters. If we drop in on a gathering, we are able to tune in very quickly, because we size up the field, tenor and mode of the situation and at once form an idea of what is likely to be being meant. In this way we know what semantic configurations—what register—will probably be required if we are to take part. If we did not do this, there would be no communication, since only a part of the meanings we have to understand are explicitly realized in the wordings. The rest are unrealized; they are left out—or rather (a more satisfactory metaphor) they are out of focus. We succeed in the exchange of meanings because we have access to the semiotic structure of the situation from other sources. (ibid., p. 189)

Knowledge of register is not used in any substantial or systematic way by current natural-language understanding systems. Some systems use knowledge of the world to resolve the ambiguity of input texts (e.g. Winograd, 1972), and other systems use knowledge of discourse structure and intentions (Grosz and Sidner, 1985). But these are not using knowledge of what linguistic devices are specific to what social situations. Winograd's program does not take advantage of the fact that there are very specific English constructs used to describe the relations between objects like blocks and the operations that are performed on sets of these objects (knowledge of field).[6]

Neither does Winograd's program take advantage of the relationship between the "robot" and the interlocutor (knowledge of tenor). The program should, to use a simple example, be expecting imperatives. Some systems (e.g. Sullivan and Cohen, 1985) use knowledge of the relationship between the speaker and hearer to make inferences about the speaker's intentions. However, these systems do not use knowledge of the specific linguistic constructs likely to appear as a result of this relationship.

Similarly, using knowledge of discourse patterns is not the same as using knowledge of which patterns of discourse are used in which types of social situations (knowledge of mode—for instance, knowledge of the ellipsis that is used heavily in question and answer dialogues). Knowledge of the most likely types of reference in particular situations would also be useful.

Unlike text generation, the parsing interface works both ways—the results of the parse must be passed back up through the semantics. It may be possible to do the sort of reconstructive reasoning that MYCIN, for example, does (Hasling et al., 1984). Once a set of grammatical features has been determined, whose realization rules specify a syntactic structure corresponding to the text, the semantic stratum is examined to find semantic features compatible with the register which preselect the grammatical seed features.

Only a few natural-language understanding issues have been mentioned here and none have been examined in detail. It appears, however, that a more thorough investigation of the implications of SLANG for natural-language understanding would be worthwhile.

8.4. Conclusion

Text generation is a subfield of natural-language work that has received relatively little attention. However, as expert systems move into areas such as medicine and law, where effective natural-language communication is important, text-generation research acquires a new significance.

This book has presented a novel approach to text generation—the Systemic Linguistic Approach to Natural-language Generation (SLANG). By interpreting a systemic grammar as AI problem-solving knowledge, SLANG is able to breach one of the major obstacles in text generation, viz. how to interface computational AI problem-solving techniques with an established linguistic formalism. Thus SLANG, unlike any other approach to date, allows that text generation to be performed directly by a powerful, goal-directed AI problem solver, while the process still follows an explicit grammar written in an established linguistic formalism.

Although SLANG has been formalized and implemented, its status at best is that it has successfully undergone a preliminary investigation. Much more work will have to be done to discover the real limitations, or for that matter the real benefits, of this approach.

Appendix A
OPS5 tutorial

The OPS5 production language (Forgy, 1981; Brownston et al., 1985) was used to implement SLANG-I. The purpose of this appendix is to provide the reader with enough OPS5 background to understand the OPS5 terms and code that appear in the passages referring to the implementation

The two main components of an OPS5 production system are the *production memory*, which stores the productions themselves, and the *working memory*, which is a repository of information accessed and modified by the productions. Productions have a left-hand side (LHS) and a right-hand side (RHS). The LHS is a list of patterns which is "matched" if all the patterns are matched by working memory elements. The RHS is a list of procedure calls.

When OPS5 is running, it takes all the productions whose LHS is matched by the current working memory, selects the production which is matched by the most recent working-memory elements, and executes the procedure calls in the RHS of that production. A new set of productions whose LHS is matched is then calculated and the process repeats. This process begins with a working memory initiallized by the user, and ends when the set of productions whose LHS is matched is empty.

A.1. The left-hand side

The patterns in the LHS of productions and in working memory are of two varieties: attribute-value pairs and vectors. An attribute-value pair pattern is of the form (identifier ^a1 v1 ^a2 v2 ... ^an vn) where the order of the individual pairs ^ai vi is not significant. For instance, there may be an element in working memory (house ^colour white ^floors 2 ^rooms 10). LHS patterns matching this element must have the same identifier and some (possibly empty) subset of the attribute-value pairs in any order. For instance, (house ˆcolour white) and (house ˆrooms 10 ˆfloors 2) would match but (house ˆcolour blue) would not.

The values can be made more general through the use of the symbols "<>" (not equal), ">" (greater than), and so on. For instance (house ˆcolour <> pink), (house ˆrooms > 4 ˆfloors < 4) would match the description of the house above, but (house ˆrooms < 8) would not. Disjunction can be specified with double angle brackets "<<" and ">>"—e.g. (house ˆcolour << green white red >> ˆfloors << 1 2 >>) would match elements describing green, white, or red houses with either one or two floors.

OPS5 rules look like

```
(p production-name
   LHS
 -->
   RHS)
```

So an actual production might begin:

```
(p eg1
   (house ˆcolour << red white >> ˆrooms > 6)
 -->
   ...
```

The LHS of the production above would be satisfied if there is an element in working memory describing a red or white house with more than 6 rooms.

It is usually necessary to have variables in productions to link the different patterns in the LHS and to mediate between the LHS and the RHS. Variables in OPS5 are symbols whose first and last characters are open and closed angle brackets respectively (e.g. <x>, <house1>, <new-house> etc.). The LHS of the production shown in Figure A.1 will be matched if there are elements in working memory describing a house, and a customer who is older than 25, whose eyes are the same colour as the house, and who has fewer children than the number of rooms of the house. Several constraints can be put on a value using curly brackets "{}". For instance, the pattern shown in Figure A.2 will match a working-memory element describing a house which is not blue or red and has between 6 and 11 rooms—setting the variable <house-colour> to whatever the actual colour is, and setting the variable <house-rooms> to whatever the

```
(p eg2
  (house        ^colour <house-colour>
                ^rooms <house-rooms>)
  (customer     ^age > 25
                ^eyes <house-colour>
                ^children < <house-rooms>)
 -->
  ...
```

Figure A.1.

```
(house ^colour {<> blue <> red <house-colour>}
       ^rooms {< 12 <house-rooms> > 5})
```

Figure A.2.

number of rooms is.

The other type of pattern used in OPS5 is the vector. In this case there are no attributes; the vector is simply a list of values where order *is* important. A LHS vector pattern with *n* symbols is matched by a working-memory vector whose first *n* elements match those of the pattern. The vector (roses are << red black >> and <flowers> are <colour2>) is matched by (roses are red and violets are blue), (roses are black), and (roses).

A.2. The right-hand side

The RHS of an OPS5 production is a list of procedure calls of the form (procedure arg1 arg2 ...). The procedure must be a built-in OPS5 procedure. The procedures used in SLANG are "make," "modify," "remove," and "call."

The procedure "make" is used to add an element (attribute-value or vector) to working memory. For instance, (make house ^colour white ^rooms 10 ^floors 2) and (make roses are red) add the working-memory elements (house ^colour white ^rooms 10 ^floors 2) and (roses are red) respectively.

The procedure "modify" is used to change an existing element in working memory. The part to be modified is specified by an attribute in the case of attribute-value pairs, or an index number in the case of vectors. The working-memory element to be modified is identified by the number of the LHS pattern it matches (1 to modify a match of the first pattern, 2 to modify a match of the second pattern and so on) or a label on the pattern. For instance if the patterns of the production shown in Figure A.3 are matched by (house ^id house3 ^colour white) and (paint house3 black), and if OPS5 fires this production, then these

```
(p eg3
  (house ^id <h>)
  (paint <h> <new-colour>)
-->
  (modify 1 ^colour <new-colour>)
  (modify 2 ^1 painted))
```

Figure A.3.

working-memory elements will be changed to (house ^id house3 ^colour black) and (painted house3 black). The same production could also be written using labels on the patterns as shown in Figure A.4.

```
(p eg3
  {(house ^id <h>)                              <house>}
  {(paint <h> <new-colour>)                     <paint>}
-->
  (modify <house> ^colour <new-colour>)
  (modify <paint> ^1 painted))
```

Figure A.4.

Here <house> and <paint> above are "element variables" that represent the entire working-memory element that matches the pattern.

The procedure "remove" simply deletes a working-memory element identified in either of the ways described above for "modify"—e.g. (remove 2) or (remove <paint>).

The procedure "call" is used to call a procedure the user has defined in another language (e.g. LISP). The parameter-passing conventions are awkward to explain, but the parameters themselves are either identifiers, variables, or the results of function calls (see below). The procedures do not pass back values, but access working memory directly through some special routines provided by OPS5.

The procedure "write" simply writes its arguments to the terminal. It too takes identifiers, variables and function calls as arguments. The function often called from "write" is "crlf," which prints a carriage return at the terminal.

Besides "crlf," the only other functions called in SLANG-I are "substr" and "genatom." The function "substr" returns a substring of an element matched in the LHS. The only call on this function is (call PRESELECT (substr <preselect> 1 inf)), which passes the entire working-memory element—string elements 1 to infinity—matching the element variable <preselect> to the LISP operator PRESELECT. The function "genatom" takes no arguments and returns a unique identifier—this is essentially the same as "gensym" in LISP.

Appendix B
Sample texts

The following are some examples of the text produced by SLANG-I (parts of the grammar used are in Appendix C). Recall that SLANG-I was not provided with an orthographic stratum, so there are no "an"s, punctuation or capitalization— except as provided by the systems at the word rank (the dictionary). To avoid confusion, line spacing has been added in lieu of punctuation where necessary.

In all cases SLANG-I generates the text one clause at a time. Although some of the samples are of paragraph length, it should not be inferred that SLANG-I has done any text planning; all the examples are collections of clauses which, as far as SLANG-I is concerned, were generated independently.

B.1. Explanation for a hypothetical expert system
The following example was generated to demonstrate the grammar, and to illustrate the utility of flexible natural-language generation in expert systems.

Suppose there is a hypothetical medical expert system interviewing the mother of a patient named Mary (following an example in Hasling et al., 1984). The mother has reported that Mary has been suffering from stiff neck muscles and headaches. At this point the hypothetical dialogue continues:

Does Mary have a fever?
*WHY

Mary's mother wants to know why she is being asked this question. The following text was generated by preselecting the grammatical features by hand. The construction of a good semantic stratum in this domain would be a major project in itself.

> well Mary has been having headaches
>
> on this basis perhaps she has a infection
>
> this possibility would be supported by a fever
>
> so we ask
>
> does she have one

The preselections for each of the clauses is as follows:

Clause 1: *well Mary has been having headaches*

```
($C1<Carrier<Head : !mary)
($C1<Carrier : non-possessive-nom)
($C1<Carrier : noun)
($C1<Carrier : non-determined)
($C1<Carrier : non-quantified)
($C1<Carrier : singular)
```

```
($C1<Attribute<Head : !headache)
($C1<Attribute : plural)
($C1<Attribute : noun)
($C1<Attribute : non-determined)
($C1<Attribute : non-quantified)
($C1<Attribute : non-possessive-nom)
```

```
($C1 : possessive-attribute)
($C1 : ascriptive)
($C1 : range-operative)
($C1 : residual)
($C1 : present)
($C1 : past-in)
($C1 : present-in)
($C1 : unmarked-declarative-theme)
($C1 : singular-subject)
($C1 : nominal-subject)
($C1 : non-attitudinal)
($C1 : textual-theme)
($C1 : responsive/explanative)
($C1 : unmarked-positive)
($C1 : non-place)
($C1 : non-time)
```

Clause 2: *on this basis perhaps she has a infection*

($C2<Carrier<Head : !feminine)
($C2<Carrier : non-possessive-nom)
($C2<Carrier : personal)
($C2<Carrier : singular)

($C2<Attribute<Head : !infection)
($C2<Attribute : singular)
($C2<Attribute : noun)
($C2<Attribute : determined)
($C2<Attribute : non-add)
($C2<Attribute : non-quantified)
($C2<Attribute : non-possessive-nom)
($C2<Attitude : !obvious)
($C2<Attitude : !low)

($C2 : possessive-attribute)
($C2 : ascriptive)
($C2 : pronominal-subject)
($C2 : range-operative)
($C2 : residual)
($C2 : present)
($C2 : non-past-in)
($C2 : non-present-in)
($C2 : unmarked-declarative-theme)
($C2 : singular-subject)
($C2 : pronominal-subject)
($C2 : non-place)
($C2 : non-time)
($C2 : interpersonal-theme)
($C2 : textual-theme)
($C2 : prop-reason)
($C2 : unmarked-positive)

Clause 3: *this possibility would be supported by a fever*

($C3<Medium : noun)
($C3<Medium : singular)
($C3<Medium : determined)
($C3<Medium : non-quantified)
($C3<Medium : non-possessive-nom)
($C3<Medium : non-add)
($C3<Medium<Head : !fever)

($C3<Process : !support)

($C3<Range : noun)
($C3<Range : singular)
($C3<Range : determined)
($C3<Range : non-quantified)
($C3<Range : near)
($C3<Range<Head : !possibility)
($C3<Range : non-possessive-nom)

($C3<Modal : !would)

($C3 : non-past-in)
($C3 : non-present-in)
($C3 : unmarked-positive)
($C3 : modal)
($C3 : unmarked-declarative-theme)
($C3 : non-attitudinal)
($C3 : non-textual-theme)
($C3 : mediated)
($C3 : residual)
($C3 : singular-subject)
($C3 : nominal-subject)
($C3 : non-place)
($C3 : non-time)

Clause 4: *so we ask*

    ($C4 : speaker-plus-subject)
    ($C4 : unmarked-positive)
    ($C4 : unmarked-declarative-theme)
    ($C4 : non-attitudinal)
    ($C4 : textual-theme)
    ($C4 : residual)
    ($C4 : interrogating)
    ($C4 : gen-simple)
    ($C4 : prop-causal)
    ($C4 : present)
    ($C4 : non-past-in)
    ($C4 : non-present-in)
    ($C4 : non-place)
    ($C4 : non-time)

    ($C4<Process : !ask)

Clause 5: *does she have one*

    ($C4<Beta : present)
    ($C4<Beta : non-past-in)
    ($C4<Beta : residual)
    ($C4<Beta : non-present-in)
    ($C4<Beta : singular-subject)
    ($C4<Beta : range-operative)
    ($C4<Beta : unmarked-yes/no-theme)
    ($C4<Beta : non-textual-theme)
    ($C4<Beta : ascriptive)
    ($C4<Beta : possessive-attribute)
    ($C4<Beta : unmarked-positive)
    ($C4<Beta : pronominal-subject)
    ($C4<Beta : non-place)
    ($C4<Beta : non-time)

    ($C4<Beta<Carrier : non-possesive-nom)
    ($C4<Beta<Carrier : personal)
    ($C4<Beta<Carrier : singular)
    ($C4<Beta<Carrier<Head : !feminine)

    ($C4<Beta<Attribute : non-possessive-nom)
    ($C4<Beta<Attribute : singular)
    ($C4<Beta<Attribute : non-determined)
    ($C4<Beta<Attribute : non-quantified)
    ($C4<Beta<Attribute : substitute)

B.2. Sample explanation of a plan

The following text was generated as part of a project to automatically generate explanations of plans. The program that did the plan analysis and text planning (Sothcott, 1985) also does the semantic reasoning, so again only the grammatical stratum was used by SLANG-I. In this case the planner is explaining the plan to one of the plan participants who is responsible for the sanding, painting and varnishing.

> first you do the painting
>
> at the same time the basement floor is poured
>
> at the same time the plasterer fastens the plaster board
>
> if the basement floor has been poured
> and the plaster board has been fastened
> then the finished flooring can be laid
>
> after that the carpentry can be finished
>
> if the carpentry has been finished
> and you've done the painting
> then you can sand the floors
>
> after that you can varnish the floors

The text planner EXPLAN (Sothcott, 1985) begins by running a scheduler that examines the output of a planner and produces a schedule of the planned actions to be described. The text planner then decides what sort of description should be given for each of these actions. The result is a blueprint for the entire text in terms of a high-level description for each clause. The text planner then fills the functional-role slots for each clause using domain-specific knowledge and input from the user. Based on relationships between these functional roles (e.g. if the Actor and the Subject match), and domain-specific knowledge about processes and entities (e.g. knowledge that "carpentry" is a mass entity), it preselects appropriate grammatical features. The following are the preselection lists for the above example as generated by EXPLAN (with very slight modifications to allow them to run on a later version of the grammar).

```
(comment
Addressee: painter
Discourse type: actor_focussed

)

(comment

Node number: 9
Sentence number: 1
Clause number: 1
Clause type: core
Topical theme: painter
Subject: painter
Voice: operative
Case frame:
        [Goal painting]
        [Process do]
        [Actor painter]


)

($C<Goal<Head : !painting)
($C<Goal : non-possessive-nom)
($C<Goal : non-quantified)
($C<Goal : non-selective)
($C<Goal : determined)
($C<Goal : noun)
($C<Goal : mass)
($C<Process : !-do-)
($C : unmarked-imperative-theme)
($C : imperative-subject-explicit)
($C : dispositive)
($C : non-benefactive)
($C : residual)
($C : operative)
($C : unmarked-positive)
($C : non-attitudinal)
($C : present)
($C : non-present-in)
($C : non-past-in)
($C : thesis-initial)
($C : textual-theme)
($C : non-place)
;--------------------------------------
```

(comment

Node number: 5
Sentence number: 2
Clause number: 2
Clause type: core
Topical theme: basement_floor
Subject: basement_floor
Voice: non-agentive (passive)
Case frame:
  [Goal basement_floor]
  [Process pour]
  [Actor unknown]

)

($C < Goal < Head : !basement-floor)
($C < Goal : non-possessive-nom)
($C < Goal : non-quantified)
($C < Goal : non-selective)
($C < Goal : determined)
($C < Goal : noun)
($C < Goal : singular)
($C < Process : !pour)
($C : unmarked-declarative-theme)
($C : singular-subject)
($C : nominal-subject)
($C : creative)
($C : non-benefactive)
($C : non-residual)
($C : non-agentive)
($C : unmarked-positive)
($C : non-attitudinal)
($C : non-present-in)
($C : non-past-in)
($C : present)
($C : thesis-simultaneous)
($C : textual-theme)
($C : non-place)
;-------------------------------------

(comment

Node number: 4
Sentence number: 3
Clause number: 3
Clause type: core
Topical theme: plasterer
Subject: plasterer
Voice: operative
Case frame:
    [Goal plaster_board]
    [Process fasten]
    [Actor plasterer]

)

($C<Goal<Head : !plaster-board)
($C<Goal : non-possessive-nom)
($C<Goal : non-quantified)
($C<Goal : non-selective)
($C<Goal : determined)
($C<Goal : noun)
($C<Goal : mass)
($C<Actor<Head : !plasterer)
($C<Actor : non-possessive-nom)
($C<Actor : non-quantified)
($C<Actor : non-selective)
($C<Actor : determined)
($C<Actor : noun)
($C<Actor : singular)
($C<Process : !fasten)
($C : unmarked-declarative-theme)
($C : singular-subject)
($C : nominal-subject)
($C : dispositive)
($C : non-benefactive)
($C : residual)
($C : operative)
($C : unmarked-positive)
($C : non-attitudinal)
($C : non-present-in)
($C : non-past-in)
($C : present)
($C : thesis-simultaneous)
($C : textual-theme)
($C : non-place)
;---------------------------------------

(comment

Node number: 5
Sentence number: 4
Clause number: 4
Clause type: subsidiary
Topical theme: basement_floor
Subject: basement_floor
Voice: non-agentive (passive)
Case frame:
      [Goal basement_floor]
      [Process pour]
      [Actor unknown]

)

($C<Goal<Head : !basement-floor)
($C<Goal : non-possessive-nom)
($C<Goal : non-quantified)
($C<Goal : non-selective)
($C<Goal : determined)
($C<Goal : noun)
($C<Goal : singular)
($C<Process : !pour)
($C : unmarked-declarative-theme)
($C : singular-subject)
($C : nominal-subject)
($C : creative)
($C : non-benefactive)
($C : non-residual)
($C : non-agentive)
($C : unmarked-positive)
($C : non-attitudinal)
($C : thesis-conditional)
($C : cond-antecedent)
($C : present)
($C : past-in)
($C : non-present-in)
($C : textual-theme)
($C : non-place)
($C : non-time)
;--

(comment

Node number: 4
Sentence number: 4
Clause number: 5
Clause type: subsidiary
Topical theme: plaster_board
Subject: plaster_board
Voice: non-agentive (passive)
Case frame:
    [Goal plaster_board]
    [Process fasten]
    [Actor plasterer]

)

($C < Goal < Head : !plaster-board)
($C < Goal : non-possessive-nom)
($C < Goal : non-quantified)
($C < Goal : non-selective)
($C < Goal : determined)
($C < Goal : noun)
($C < Goal : mass)
($C < Process : !fasten)
($C : unmarked-declarative-theme)
($C : mass-subject)
($C : nominal-subject)
($C : dispositive)
($C : non-benefactive)
($C : non-residual)
($C : non-agentive)
($C : unmarked-positive)
($C : non-attitudinal)
($C : simp-add)
($C : present)
($C : past-in)
($C : non-present-in)
($C : textual-theme)
($C : non-place)
($C : non-time)
;------------------------------------

(comment

Node number: 6
Sentence number: 4
Clause number: 6
Clause type: core
Topical theme: finished_flooring
Subject: finished_flooring
Voice: non-agentive (passive)
Case frame:
    [Goal finished_flooring]
    [Process lay]
    [Actor unknown]

)

($C<Goal<Head : !finished-flooring)
($C<Goal : non-possessive-nom)
($C<Goal : non-quantified)
($C<Goal : non-selective)
($C<Goal : determined)
($C<Goal : noun)
($C<Goal : mass)
($C<Process : !lay)
($C : unmarked-declarative-theme)
($C : mass-subject)
($C : nominal-subject)
($C : dispositive)
($C : non-benefactive)
($C : non-residual)
($C : non-agentive)
($C : unmarked-positive)
($C : non-attitudinal)
($C : thesis-conditional)
($C : cond-simple)
($C : textual-theme)
($C<Modal : !can)
($C : modal)
($C : non-past-in)
($C : non-present-in)
($C : non-place)
($C : non-time)
;--------------------------------------

(comment

Node number: 7
Sentence number: 5
Clause number: 7
Clause type: core
Topical theme: carpentry
Subject: carpentry
Voice: non-agentive (passive)
Case frame:
        [Goal carpentry]
        [Process finish]
        [Actor unknown]

)

($C < Goal < Head : !carpentry)
($C < Goal : non-possessive-nom)
($C < Goal : non-quantified)
($C < Goal : non-selective)
($C < Goal : determined)
($C < Goal : noun)
($C < Goal : mass)
($C < Process : !finish)
($C : unmarked-declarative-theme)
($C : mass-subject)
($C : nominal-subject)
($C : dispositive)
($C : non-benefactive)
($C : non-residual)
($C : non-agentive)
($C : unmarked-positive)
($C : non-attitudinal)
($C : thesis-succeeding)
($C : textual-theme)
($C < Modal : !can)
($C : modal)
($C : non-past-in)
($C : non-present-in)
($C : non-place)
;----------------------------------

```
(comment

Node number: 7
Sentence number: 6
Clause number: 8
Clause type: subsidiary
Topical theme: carpentry
Subject: carpentry
Voice: non-agentive  (passive)
Case frame:
      [Goal carpentry]
      [Process finish]
      [Actor unknown]


)

($C<Goal<Head : !carpentry)
($C<Goal : non-possessive-nom)
($C<Goal : non-quantified)
($C<Goal : non-selective)
($C<Goal : determined)
($C<Goal : noun)
($C<Goal : mass)
($C<Process : !finish)
($C : unmarked-declarative-theme)
($C : mass-subject)
($C : nominal-subject)
($C : dispositive)
($C : non-benefactive)
($C : non-residual)
($C : non-agentive)
($C : unmarked-positive)
($C : non-attitudinal)
($C : thesis-conditional)
($C : cond-antecedent)
($C : present)
($C : past-in)
($C : non-present-in)
($C : textual-theme)
($C : non-place)
($C : non-time)
;------------------------------------
```

(comment

Node number: 9
Sentence number: 6
Clause number: 9
Clause type: subsidiary
Topical theme: painter
Subject: painter
Voice: operative
Case frame:
      [Goal painting]
      [Process do]
      [Actor painter]

)

($C < Goal < Head : !painting)
($C < Goal : non-possessive-nom)
($C < Goal : non-quantified)
($C < Goal : non-selective)
($C < Goal : determined)
($C < Goal : noun)
($C < Goal : mass)
($C < Process : !-do-)
($C : unmarked-declarative-theme)
($C : addressee-subject)
($C : dispositive)
($C : non-benefactive)
($C : residual)
($C : operative)
($C : unmarked-positive)
($C : non-attitudinal)
($C : simp-add)
($C : present)
($C : past-in)
($C : non-present-in)
($C : textual-theme)
($C : non-place)
($C : non-time)
;---------------------------------------

(comment

Node number: 8
Sentence number: 6
Clause number: 10
Clause type: core
Topical theme: painter
Subject: painter
Voice: operative
Case frame:
     [Goal floors]
     [Process sand]
     [Actor painter]

)

($C<Goal<Head : !floor)
($C<Goal : non-possessive-nom)
($C<Goal : non-quantified)
($C<Goal : non-selective)
($C<Goal : determined)
($C<Goal : noun)
($C<Goal : plural)
($C<Process : !sand)
($C : unmarked-declarative-theme)
($C : addressee-subject)
($C : dispositive)
($C : non-benefactive)
($C : residual)
($C : operative)
($C : unmarked-positive)
($C : non-attitudinal)
($C : thesis-conditional)
($C : cond-simple)
($C : textual-theme)
($C<Modal : !can)
($C : modal)
($C : non-past-in)
($C : non-present-in)
($C : non-place)
($C : non-time)
;---------------------------------------

(comment

Node number: 2
Sentence number: 7
Clause number: 11
Clause type: core
Topical theme: painter
Subject: painter
Voice: operative
Case frame:
       [Goal floors]
       [Process varnish]
       [Actor painter]

)

($C<Goal<Head : !floor)
($C<Goal : non-possessive-nom)
($C<Goal : non-quantified)
($C<Goal : non-selective)
($C<Goal : determined)
($C<Goal : noun)
($C<Goal : plural)
($C<Process : !varnish)
($C : unmarked-declarative-theme)
($C : addressee-subject)
($C : dispositive)
($C : non-benefactive)
($C : residual)
($C : operative)
($C : unmarked-positive)
($C : non-attitudinal)
($C : thesis-succeeding)
($C : textual-theme)
($C<Modal : !can)
($C : modal)
($C : non-past-in)
($C : non-present-in)
($C : non-place)
;------------------------------------

The interface and compiled knowledge embodied in EXPLAN can be extracted to form a semantic system network for this domain. The blueprint for the text would be constructed exactly as before, but now the text planning of the individual clauses would end by simply setting features of the semantic stratum as goals.

The semantic system network contains the systems shown in Figure B.1 (due to space restrictions, only two gates—*builder-mentioned* and *builder-unmentioned*—have been included in the diagram. The complete network including gates and realization rules can be found in Appendix C, §C.11).

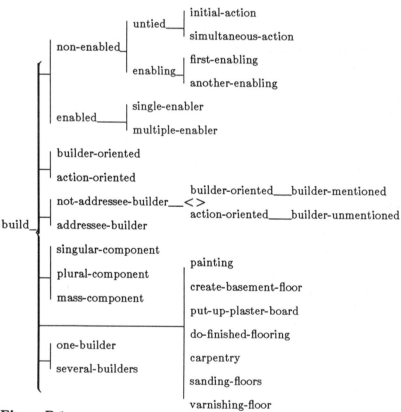

Figure B.1.

When text planning for a particular action on the schedule, the text planner may decide to describe the other actions that enabled the action in question. When constructing the blueprint for a series of descriptions of enabling actions followed by a description of the enabled action, the planner simply sets goals such as $first-enabling (for the first of the enabling actions) and $multiple-enablers (for the enabled action). If the addressee of the text is the person that is performing the action, then the goal $addressee-builder is set, otherwise $not-addressee-builder is set. The text planner need not assign grammatical functional roles—that will be done by the grammar. Using the same type of reasoning already done by EXPLAN, the text planner can set the appropriate goals for the number of the component being operated upon, and the operation itself. The EXPLAN choice between Actor-focused and Goal-focused is simply replaced by the choice between $builder-oriented and $action-oriented.

The input SLANG now requires to generate the example is as follows (in each case the semantic features are associated with the top-level hub—by convention hub 0):

first you do the painting

```
(make goal $initial-action 0)
(make goal $action-oriented 0)
(make goal $addressee-builder 0)
(make goal $mass-component 0)
(make goal $one-builder 0)
(make goal $painting 0)
```

at the same time the basement floor is poured

```
(make goal $simultaneous-action 0)
(make goal $action-oriented 0)
(make goal $not-addressee-builder 0)
(make goal $singular-component 0)
(make goal $one-builder 0)
(make goal $create-basement-floor 0)
```

at the same time the plasterer fastens the plaster board

```
(make goal $simultaneous-action 0)
(make goal $builder-oriented 0)
(make goal $not-addressee-builder 0)
(make goal $mass-component 0)
(make goal $one-builder 0)
(make goal $put-up-plaster-board 0)
```

if the basement floor has been poured

```
(make goal $first-enabling 0)
(make goal $action-oriented 0)
(make goal $not-addressee-builder 0)
(make goal $singular-component 0)
(make goal $one-builder 0)
(make goal $create-basement-floor 0)
```

and the plaster board has been fastened

```
(make goal $another-enabling 0)
(make goal $action-oriented 0)
(make goal $not-addressee-builder 0)
(make goal $mass-component 0)
(make goal $one-builder 0)
(make goal $put-up-plaster-board 0)
```

then the finished flooring can be laid

```
(make goal $multiple-enabler 0)
(make goal $action-oriented 0)
(make goal $not-addressee-builder 0)
(make goal $mass-component 0)
(make goal $one-builder 0)
(make goal $do-finished-flooring 0)
```

after that the carpentry can be finished

```
(make goal $single-enabler 0)
(make goal $action-oriented 0)
(make goal $not-addressee-builder 0)
(make goal $mass-component 0)
(make goal $one-builder 0)
(make goal $carpentry 0)
```

if the carpentry has been finished

```
(make goal $first-enabling 0)
(make goal $action-oriented 0)
(make goal $not-addressee-builder 0)
(make goal $mass-component 0)
(make goal $one-builder 0)
(make goal $carpentry 0)
```

and you've done the painting

```
(make goal $another-enabling 0)
(make goal $action-oriented 0)
(make goal $addressee-builder 0)
(make goal $mass-component 0)
(make goal $one-builder 0)
(make goal $painting 0)
```

then you can sand the floors

```
(make goal $multiple-enabler 0)
(make goal $action-oriented 0)
(make goal $addressee-builder 0)
(make goal $plural-component 0)
(make goal $one-builder 0)
(make goal $sanding-floor 0)
```

after that you can varnish the floors

```
(make goal $single-enabler 0)
(make goal $action-oriented 0)
(make goal $addressee-builder 0)
(make goal $plural-component 0)
(make goal $one-builder 0)
(make goal $varnishing-floor 0)
```

There are some important advantages to using a semantic system network as an interface between the text planner and the grammar. The linguistic notation developed expressly for this purpose makes it easier to perceive the grammatically relevant decisions and how they are realized. The modularity of the language production is improved since the text planner is not required to know about grammatical features and functional roles.

B.3. Examples from the semantic stratum

The following samples were generated using the semantic stratum (based on Halliday, 1978, pp. 82-4), which is listed at the end of Appendix C. The register involves a mother attempting to control the behaviour of her child with a threat.

Each example consists of an input to SLANG-I (a set of semantic seed features to be set as goals), preceded by the resulting text. In each case the features are associated with the top-level hub—by convention hub 0.

you'll be going upstairs

(make goal $rejection 0)
(make goal $at-home 0)
(make goal $child-centred-decision 0)
(make goal $deferred 0)

you're going upstairs

(make goal $rejection 0)
(make goal $at-home 0)
(make goal $child-centred-decision 0)
(make goal $pending 0)
(make goal $unmarked-time 0)

I'm taking you upstairs now

(make goal $rejection 0)
(make goal $at-home 0)
(make goal $mother-centred-decision 0)
(make goal $pending 0)
(make goal $immediate 0)

I'll smack you

(make goal $unconditional 0)
(make goal $chastisement 0)
(make goal $smack 0)
(make goal $adult-centred-punishment 0)

you mustn't do that because I'll smack you

(make goal $threatening-reason 0)
(make goal $non-repetitive 0)
(make goal $chastisement 0)
(make goal $smack 0)
(make goal $explanatory-cond 0)
(make goal $adult-centred-punishment 0)

if you do that I'll smack you

(make goal $logical-cond 0)
(make goal $non-repetitive 0)
(make goal $chastisement 0)
(make goal $smack 0)
(make goal $adult-centred-punishment 0)

don't do that
next time I'll smack you

(make goal $straight-threat 0)
(make goal $explicit-repetition 0)
(make goal $chastisement 0)
(make goal $smack 0)
(make goal $exclamatory-cond 0)
(make goal $adult-centred-punishment 0)

go upstalrs now

(make goal $unmarked-command 0)
(make goal $immediate 0)
(make goal $at-home 0)

you'll be smacked

(make goal $unconditional 0)
(make goal $chastisement 0)
(make goal $smack 0)
(make goal $child-centred-punishment 0)

you mustn't do that or you'll be smacked

(make goal $threatening-alternative 0)
(make goal $non-repetitive 0)
(make goal $chastisement 0)
(make goal $smack 0)
(make goal $explanatory-cond 0)
(make goal $child-centred-punishment 0)

don't do that or you'll be smacked by Daddy

(make goal $threatening-alternative 0)
(make goal $non-repetitive 0)
(make goal $daddy 0)
(make goal $smack 0)
(make goal $exclamatory-cond 0)
(make goal $child-centred-punishment 0)

you mustn't do that
next time I'll smack you

(make goal $straight-threat 0)
(make goal $explicit-repetition 0)
(make goal $chastisement 0)
(make goal $smack 0)
(make goal $explanatory-cond 0)
(make goal $adult-centred-punishment 0)

I am not giving you a sweet

(make goal $deprivation 0)
(make goal $at-home 0)
(make goal $mother-centred-decision 0)
(make goal $pending 0)
(make goal $unmarked-time 0)

you are not being given a sweet

(make goal $deprivation 0)
(make goal $at-home 0)
(make goal $child-centred-decision 0)
(make goal $pending 0)
(make goal $unmarked-time 0)

you will not be being given a sweet

(make goal $deprivation 0)
(make goal $at-home 0)
(make goal $child-centred-decision 0)
(make goal $deferred 0)

I will not be giving you a sweet

```
(make goal $deprivation 0)
(make goal $at-home 0)
(make goal $mother-centred-decision 0)
(make goal $deferred 0)
```

Appendix C
Excerpts from the grammar

This appendix contains excerpts from the grammar used in the implementation, and used to generate the sample texts in Appendix B. The networks were collected from a variety of sources, and patched together when necessary. No attempt has been made to develop a polished grammar—there are several dubious fixes and no doubt many outright errors and omissions. This grammar was intended only to test the ideas described in this book.

The notation used here is a LISP-based system network notation described in §6.2.1.

C.1. Excerpts from the clause network

The clause network was based on Mann/Halliday, an early version of the clause network for Nigel (Mann et al., 1983).

(nil CLAUSE)

((CLAUSE -[) **clause**
    (Process / Lexverb) (# ˆ Theme))

((clause -{=) MOOD)

((MOOD -[) **finite**
    (Mood (Finite)) (Mood ˆ Residue))

((finite -{=) MOOD-TYPE)

((MOOD-TYPE -[) **indicative**
    (Mood (Subject)) (Residue ˆ #))

((indicative -{=) INDICATIVE-TYPE)

((INDICATIVE-TYPE -[) **declarative**
    (Subject ˆ Finite) (% ˆ Subject) (Finite ˆ %))

((MOOD-TYPE -[) **imperative**
  (Mood (Subject)) (Process : !stem))
((indicative
  interactant-subject
  =}-) INDICATIVE-INTERACTANT-SUBJECT)

((INDICATIVE-INTERACTANT-SUBJECT -[) **speaker-subject**
  (Subject = I)
  (Finite : !first-person)
  (Finite : !v-singular))

((INDICATIVE-INTERACTANT-SUBJECT -[) **addressee-subject**
  (Subject = you) (Finite : !second-person))

((INDICATIVE-INTERACTANT-SUBJECT -[) **speaker-plus-subject**
  (Subject = we)
  (Finite : !first-person)
  (Finite : !v-plural))

((IMPERATIVE-TAG -[) **imperative-tagged**
  (Residue ^ Moodtag)
  (Moodtag ^ #)
  (Moodtag (Tagfinite))
  (Moodtag (Tagsubject))
  (Tagfinite ^ Tagsubject)
  (% ^ Tagfinite)
  (Tagsubject ^ %))

((imperative-tagged oblative =}-) **oblative-tagged**
  (Tagfinite = shall) (Tagsubject = I))

((THEME-MARKING-DECLARATIVE -[) **unmarked-declarative-theme**
  (Topical / Subject))

((EFFECTIVE-VOICE -[) operative
  (Agent / Subject) (Medium / Residual))

((EFFECTIVE-VOICE -[) **receptive**
  (Lexverb : !en))

((TEXTUAL-THEME -[) **textual-theme**
  (Theme (Textual)) (% ^ Textual) (Textual / Conjunct))

((indicative marked-negative =}-) **nonreduced-negfinite**
  (Finite : !nonreduced))

((passive-process
  (past present]-)
  non-past-in
  non-present-in
  =}-) **finitepass**
  (Finite / Pass) (% ^ Lexverb))

((present-in passive-process =}-) **ingpass**
  (Pass = being) (Ing / Pass))

(((finiteprog finitepass]-)
  present
  speaker-subject
  =}-) **am**
    (Finite : !am))

(((finiteprog finitepass]-)
  present
  (addressee-subject
   speaker-plus-subject
   plural-subject
   ]-)
  =}-) **are**
    (Finite : !are))

(((finiteprog finitepass]-)
  past
  (addressee-subject
   speaker-plus-subject
   plural-subject
   ]-)
  =}-) **were**
    (Finite : !were))

((finiteperf
  present
  (plural-subject
   speaker-subject
   addressee-subject
   speaker-plus-subject
   ]-)
  =}-) **have**
    (Finite : !have))

((circumstantial-ascription
  possessive-ascription
  active-process
  material
  mental
  verbal
  ]-) **do-needing-verbs**)

((non-assertive not-auxed do-needing-verbs =}-) **do-finite**
    (Lexverb : !stem) (% ˆ Lexverb))

((present
  do-finite
  (mass-subject singular-subject]-)
  =}-) **does**
    (Finite : !does))

C.2. Excerpts from the nominal-group network

This network was taken from Halliday (1976b, p. 131).

188

(nil **nominal-group**
    (Head ^ #))

((nominal-group -{=) CLASS-AT-HEAD)

((CLASS-AT-HEAD -[) **nominal**)

((nominal -[) **noun**)

((nominal -[) **substitute**
    (Head = one))

((non-nominal -[) **determiner-head**
    (Deictic / Head) (# ^ Deictic))

(((determiner-head pronoun]-)
    (singular mass]-)
  =}-) **sing-pro**
    (Head : !singular-pronoun))

((pronoun possessive-nom =}-) **poss-pro**
    (Head : !possessive-pronoun))

C.3. Excerpts from the determiner network

This network was taken from Halliday (1976b, pp. 132-3), with slight extensions
and modifications from Quirk, Greenbaum, Leech and Svartvik (1973, §4.122).
This network is meant to be interpreted as an extension of the nominal-group
network rather than an independent network (note the entry conditions of
DETERMINER are from the nominal-group network).

((determined determiner-head]-) DETERMINER)

((DETERMINER -[) **specific**)

((specific -[) **non-selective**
    (Deictic = the))

(((quasi-negative unrestricted]-)
    (mass plural]-)
  <>) **"any"**
    (Deictic = any))

((restricted (mass plural]-) -<>) **"some"**
    (Deictic = some))

C.4. Excerpts from the quantifier network

This network was taken from Halliday (1976b, pp. 134-5) and is also an extension
of the nominal-group network.

((quantifer -[) **indefinite**)

((comparative-quant -[) **multal3**
    (Numerative = more))

((superlative-adj -[) **multal4**
    (Numerative = most))

((superlative-adj -[) **paucal4**)

((paucal4 mass -<>) **least**
    (Numerative = least))

((paucal4 plural -<>) **fewest**
    (Numerative = fewest))

C.5. The prepositional-phrase network
This is described in Halliday (1985, pp. 189-90). This is the entire network.

(nil **prep-phrase**
    (Range : nominal-group) (Range ^ #))

((prep-phrase -[) **unmarked-prep-phrase**
    (# ^ Minor-process)
    (Minor-process ^ Range)
    (Minor-process : !preposition))

((prep-phrase -[) **merged**
    (# ^ Range))

C.6. Excerpts from the verb network
This is an integrated verb and auxiliary network, very loosely fashioned after
Winograd (1983, p. 534).

(nil **!verb**)

((!verb -{=) VERB-TYPE)

((VERB-TYPE -[) **!aux**
    (# ^ !Aux))

((!modal-aux -[) **!should**)

((!have-aux -[) **!have**)

((!aux !negnonreduced =}-) **!aux-not**
    (!Neg = not) (!Aux ^ !Neg) (!Neg ^ #))

((!am ((!positive !nonreduced =}-) !negative]-) =}-) ”**am**”
    (!Aux = am))

((!am !positive !reduced =}-) ”**m**”
    (!Aux = |’m|))

((!have !positive !reduced =}-) ”**ve**”
    (!Aux = |’ve|))

((!have !negative !reduced =}-) "**havent**"
    (!Aux = |haven't|))

((!should !negative !reduced =}-) "**shouldnt**"
    (!Aux = |shouldn't|))

((!present !third-person !v-singular =}-) !**sing3**)

((!past
 !first-person
 !second-person
 !v-plural
 ]-) !**non-sing3**)

((!-be- !stem =}-) "**-be-**"
    (!Verb = be))

((!-be- !infinitive =}-) "**to-be**"
    (!Verb = |to be|))

((!-be- !first-person !singular =}-) "**-am-**"
    (!Verb = am))

((!-be-
 !present
 (!plural (!second-person !singular =}-)]-)
 =}-) "**-are-**"
    (!Verb = are))

((!-be- !sing3 !present =}-) "**-is-**"
    (!Verb = is))

((!-be-
 !past
 (!first-person !third-person]-)
 !singular
 =}-) "**-was-**"
    (!Verb = was))

((!-be-
 !past
 ((!second-person !singular =}-)
 (!third-person !plural =}-)
 ]-)
 =}-) "**-were-**"
    (!Verb = were))

((!-be- !ing =}-) "**-being-**"
    (!Verb = being))

((!-be- !en =}-) "**-been-**"
    (!Verb = been))

((!take !infinitive =}-) "**to-take**"
    (!Verb = |to take|))

((!take !past =}-) "**took**"
    (!Verb = took))

C.7. Excerpts from the noun network

The important systems from this network were taken from Winograd (1983, p. 537).

(nil **!noun**
    (# ˆ !Noun) (!Noun ˆ #))

((!noun -[) **!pronoun**)

((!noun -[) **!proper**)

((!noun -[) **!common**)

((!singular-pronoun !first !subjective =}-) "**I**"
    (!Noun = I))

((!singular-pronoun !first !objective =}-) "**me**"
    (!Noun = me))

((!plural-pronoun !first !subjective =}-) "**we**"
    (!Noun = we))

((!plural-pronoun !first !objective =}-) "**us**"
    (!Noun = us))

((!singular-pronoun !third !subjective !masculine =}-) "**he**"
    (!Noun = he))

((!singular-pronoun !third !objective !masculine =}-) "**him**"
    (!Noun = him))

((!singular-pronoun !first !possessive-pronoun =}-) "**mine**"
    (!Noun = mine))

((!plural-pronoun !first !possessive-pronoun =}-) "**ours**"
    (!Noun = ours))

((!singular-pronoun !first !possessive-determiner =}-) "**my**"
    (!Noun = my))

((!plural-pronoun !first !possessive-determiner =}-) "**our**"
    (!Noun = our))

((!near !singular-pronoun =}-) "**this**"
    (!Noun = this))

((!near !plural-pronoun =}-) "**these**"
    (!Noun = these))

((!far !singular-pronoun =}-) "**that**"
    (!Noun = that))

((!far !plural-pronoun =}-) "**those**"
    (!Noun = those))

C.8. Excerpts from the conjunction network

This network of conjunctive expressions was based on Halliday and Hasan (1976, pp. 242-3). The least delicate systems are from the clause network of Mann/Halliday which interface well with the table of conjunctive relations in Halliday and Hasan (1976). Thus this network takes the form of an extention of the clause network rather than the separate network at the work rank.

((clause -{=) CONJUNCTION)

((CONJUNCTION-TYPE -[) **temporal-type**
    (Conjunct / Time))

((tt-simple -[) **thesis-sequential**
    (Time = then))

((tt-complex -[) **thesis-durative**
    (Time — meanwhile))

((CONJUNCTION-TYPE -[) **causal**
    (Conjunct / Causal))

((prop-respective -[) **resp-rev-polarity**
    (Causal = otherwise))

((add-apposition -|) **exemplificatory**
    (Additive = |for instance|))

((continuative -[) **responsive/explanative**
    (Cont = well))

C.9 Excerpts from the modal adjunct network

From (Halliday, 1985, p. 50).
((!admissive -[) **!honesty**
    (!Adj = |to be honest|))

C.10. Excerpts from the preposition network

This fragment of a preposition network was taken from Quirk and Greenbaum (1973, p. 146).

(nil **!preposition**
    (# ^ !Prep) (!Prep ^ #))

((!preposition -{=) **POS/NEG**)

((POS/NEG -[) **!prep-positive**)

((POS/NEG -[) !**prep-negative**)

((!preposition -{=) DIR/POS)

((DIR/POS -[) !**prep-direction**)

((DIR/POS -[) !**prep-position**)

((!preposition -{=) DIMENSION)

((DIMENSION -[) !**point**)

((DIMENSION -[) !**line/surface**)

((DIMENSION -[) !**area/volume**)

((!prep-positive !prep-direction !point =}-) "**to**"
    (!Prep = to))

((!prep-positive !prep-position !point =}-) "**at**"
    (!Prep = at))

((!prep-negative !prep-direction !point =}-) "**from**"
    (!Prep = from))

((!prep-positive !prep-direction !line/surface =}-) "**onto**"
    (!Prep = onto))

((!prep-negative !area/volume =}-) "**out-of**"
    (!Prep = |out of|))

C.11. The semantic stratum

The semantic system network presented here contains the house-building semantics (see §B.2) and the threat semantics (see §3.6, §B.3).

(nil $**emantics**)

(($emantics -[) $**build**
    (# ^ $Build)
    ($Build ^ #)
    ($Build : non-benefactive)
    ($Build : unmarked-positive)
    ($Build : non-attitudinal)
    ($Build : non-present-in)
    ($Build : textual-theme)
    ($Build : non-place)
    ($Build<Goal : non-possessive-nom)
    ($Build<Goal : determined)
    ($Build<Goal : non-quantified)
    ($Build<Goal : non-selective)
    ($Build<Goal : noun))

(($build -{=) ENABLEMENT)

194

((ENABLEMENT -[) **$non-enabled**
    ($Build : present))

(($non-enabled -[) **$untied**
    ($Build : non-past-in))

(($untied -[) **$initial-action**
    ($Build : thesis-initial))

(($untied -[) **$simultaneous-action**
    ($Build : thesis-simultaneous))

(($non-enabled -[) **$enabling**
    ($Build : past-in) ($Build : non-time))

(($enabling -[) **$first-enabling**
    ($Build : thesis-conditional) ($Build : cond-antecedent))

(($enabling -[) **$another-enabling**
    ($Build : simp-add))

((ENABLEMENT -[) **$enabled**
    ($Build : non-past-in)
    ($Build : modal)
    ($Build<Modal : !can)
    ($Build : non-time)
    ($Build : unmarked-declarative-theme))

(($enabled -[) **$single-enabler**
    ($Build : thesis-succeeding))

(($enabled -[) **$multiple-enabler**
    ($Build : thesis-conditional) ($Build : cond-simple))

(($build (−) DISCOURSE TYPE)

((DISCOURSE-TYPE -[) **$builder-oriented**
    ($Build : residual) ($Build : operative))

((DISCOURSE-TYPE -[) **$action-oriented**)

(($build -{=) ADDRESSEE)

((ADDRESSEE -[) **$not-addressee-builder**
    ($Build : unmarked-declarative-theme)
    ($Build : nominal-subject))

((ADDRESSEE -[) **$addressee-builder**
    ($Build : residual) ($Build : operative))

(($build -{=) COMPONENT-NUMBER)

((COMPONENT-NUMBER -[) **$singular-component**
    ($Build<Goal : singular))

((COMPONENT-NUMBER -[) **$plural-component**
   ($Build<Goal : plural))

((COMPONENT-NUMBER -[) **$mass-component**
   ($Build<Goal : mass))

(($build -{=) BUILDER-NUMBER)

((BUILDER-NUMBER -[) **$one-builder**)

((BUILDER-NUMBER -[) **$several-builders**)

(($build -{=) ACTION)

((ACTION -[) **$painting**
   ($Build : dispositive)
   ($Build<Process : !-do-)
   ($Build<Goal<Head : !painting))

((ACTION -[) **$create-basement-floor**
   ($Build : creative)
   ($Build<Process : !pour)
   ($Build<Goal<Head : !basement-floor))

((ACTION -[) **$put-up-plaster-board**
   ($Build : dispositive)
   ($Build<Process : !fasten)
   ($Build<Goal<Head : !plaster-board))

((ACTION -[) **$do-finished-flooring**
   ($Build : dispositive)
   ($Build<Process : !lay)
   ($Build<Goal<Head : !finished-flooring))

((ACTION -[) **$carpentry**
   ($Build : dispositive)
   ($Build<Process : !finish)
   ($Build<Goal<Head : !carpentry))

((ACTION -[) **$sanding-floor**
   ($Build : dispositive)
   ($Build<Process : !sand)
   ($Build<Goal<Head : !floor))

((ACTION -[) **$varnishing-floor**
   ($Build : dispositive)
   ($Build<Process : !varnish)
   ($Build<Goal<Head : !floor))

(($addressee-builder $untied -<>) **$addressee-command**
   ($Build : unmarked-imperative-theme)
   ($Build : imperative-subject-explicit))

(($addressee-builder ($enabled $enabling]-) -< >) **$addressee-check**
    ($Build : unmarked-declarative-theme)
    ($Build : addressee-subject))

((($builder-oriented $one-builder =}-)
 ($action-oriented $singular-component =}-)
 ]-) **$single-subject**
    ($Build : singular-subject))

((($builder-oriented $several-builders =}-)
 ($action-oriented $plural-component =}-)
 ]-) **$plural-subject**
    ($Build : plural-subject))

(($not-addressee-builder
 $action-oriented
 $mass-component
 =}-) **$mass-subject**
    ($Build : mass-subject))

(($not-addressee-builder $action-oriented -< >) **$builder-unmentioned**
    ($Build : non-agentive) ($Build : non-residual))

(($not-addressee-builder $builder-oriented -< >) **$builder-mentioned**
    ($Build<Actor : non-possessive-nom)
    ($Build<Actor : non-quantified)
    ($Build<Actor : non-selective)
    ($Build<Actor : determined)
    ($Build<Actor : noun))

(($builder-mentioned $painting =}-) **$painter**
    ($Build<Actor<Head : !painter))

(($builder-mentioned
 ($do-finished-flooring $carpentry]-)
 =}-) **$carpenter**
    ($Build<Actor<Head : !carpenter))

(($builder-mentioned $put-up-plaster-board =}-) **$plasterer**
    ($Build<Actor<Head : !plasterer))

;;; The threat semantics

;;; This simple network was taken from Halliday (1978, pp. 82-4).

(($emantics -[) **$threat**
    ($Threat : non-past-in)
    ($Threat : dispositive)
    ($Threat ^ #))

(($threat -[) **$loss-of-privilege**
    (# ^ $Threat) ($Threat : non-textual-theme))

(($loss-of-privilege -[) **$command**
    ($Threat : middle)
    ($Threat : jussive)
    ($Threat : non-benefactive)
    ($Threat : unmarked-imperative-theme)
    ($Threat : proper-subject)
    ($Threat : non-residual)
    ($Threat : non-present-in)
    ($Threat : operative)
    ($Threat : unmarked-positive)
    ($Threat : place)
    ($Threat<Process : !go))

(($command -[) **$get-attention**
    ($Threat : imperative-subject-explicit))

(($command -[) **$unmarked-command**
    ($Threat : imperative-subject-implicit))

(($loss-of-privilege -[) **$decision**
    ($Threat : unmarked-declarative-theme)
    ($Threat : non-attitudinal))

(($decision -[) **$rejection**
    ($Threat : unmarked-positive)
    ($Threat : place)
    ($Threat : non-benefactive))

(($decision -[) **$deprivation**
    ($Threat : marked-negative)
    ($Threat : non-place)
    ($Threat : residual)
    ($Threat<Process : !give)
    ($Threat<Medium : non-possessive-nom)
    ($Threat<Medium : singular)
    ($Threat<Medium : noun)
    ($Threat<Medium : non-quantified)
    ($Threat<Medium : determined)
    ($Threat<Medium : non-add)
    ($Threat<Medium<Head : !sweet))

(($decision -[) **$resolution**
    ($Threat : present-in))

(($decision -[) **$obligation**
    ($Threat : passive-modulation) ($Threat : necessary))

(($decision -[) **$mother-centred-decision**
    ($Threat : speaker-subject) ($Threat : operative))

(($decision -[) **$child-centred-decision**
    ($Threat : addressee-subject))

(($resolution -[) **$pending**
    ($Threat : present))

((($pending $command]-) -[) **$unmarked-time**
    ($Threat : non-time))

((($pending $command]-) -[) **$immediate**
    ($Threat : non-textual-time)
    ($Threat<Temporal : !now))

(($resolution -[) **$deferred**
    ($Threat : future) ($Threat : non-time))

(($emantics -[) **$at-home**)

(($threat -[) **$punishment**
    ($Threat : non-benefactive)
    ($Threat : unmarked-declarative-theme)
    ($Threat : non-place)
    ($Threat : non-attitudinal)
    ($Threat : non-present-in)
    ($Threat : residual)
    ($Threat : unmarked-positive)
    ($Threat : future))

(($punishment -[) **$adult-centred-punishment**
    ($Threat : operative)
    ($Threat<Goal : non-possessive-nom)
    ($Threat<Goal : personal)
    ($Threat<Goal : singular)
    ($Threat<Goal<Head : !second)
    ($Threat<Goal<Head : !objective))

(($punishment -[) **$child-centred-punishment**
    ($Threat : addressee-subject))

(($punishment -[) **$chastisement**)

(($punishment -[) **$authority-figure**
    ($Threat<Actor : non-possessive-nom)
    ($Threat<Actor : noun))

(($punishment -[) **$unconditional**
    (# ^ $Threat) ($Threat : non-textual-theme))

(($punishment -[) **$conditional**
    (# ˆ $Cond)
    ($Cond ˆ $Threat)
    ($Cond : non-benefactive)
    ($Cond : non-place)
    ($Cond : non-time)
    ($Cond : addressee-subject)
    ($Cond : operative)
    ($Cond : residual)
    ($Cond : non-past-in)
    ($Cond : non-present-in)
    ($Cond : dispositive)
    ($Cond<Process : !-do-)
    ($Cond<Goal : non-possessive-nom)
    ($Cond<Goal : singular)
    ($Cond<Goal : determiner-head)
    ($Cond<Goal : far))

(($conditional -[) **$explicit-repetition**)

(($conditional -[) **$non-repetitive**
    ($Threat : non-time))

(($conditional -[) **$logical-cond**
    ($Cond : textual-theme)
    ($Threat : non-textual-theme)
    ($Cond : thesis-conditional)
    ($Cond : cond-antecedent)
    ($Cond : unmarked-positive)
    ($Cond : present))

(($conditional -[) **$non-logical-cond**
    ($Threat : textual-theme)
    ($Cond : non-textual-theme)
    ($Cond : unmarked-negative))

(($non-logical-cond -[) **$threatening-reason**
    ($Threat : reversed-causal))

(($non-logical-cond -[) **$threatening-alternative**
    ($Threat : simp-alternative))

(($non-logical-cond -[) **$straight-threat**)

(($non-logical-cond -[) **$exclamatory-cond**
    ($Cond : unmarked-imperative-theme)
    ($Cond : proper-subject)
    ($Cond : imperative-subject-implicit))

(($non-logical-cond -[) **$explanatory-cond**
    ($Cond : modal)
    ($Cond : addressee-subject)
    ($Cond<Modal : !must))

((\$deprivation
  \$mother-centred-decision
 -< >) **\$mother-deprivation**
    (\$Threat : ben-med)
    (\$Threat<Beneficiary : non-possessive-nom)
    (\$Threat<Beneficiary : personal)
    (\$Threat<Beneficiary : singular)
    (\$Threat<Beneficiary<Head : !second)
    (\$Threat<Beneficiary<Head : !objective))

((\$deprivation
  \$child-centred-decision
 -< >) **\$child-deprivation**
    (\$Threat : non-agentive) (\$Threat : benereceptive))

((\$rejection
  \$mother-centred-decision
 -< >) **\$mother-rejection**
    (\$Threat : residual)
    (\$Threat<Process : !take)
    (\$Threat<Goal : non-possessive-nom)
    (\$Threat<Goal : personal)
    (\$Threat<Goal : singular)
    (\$Threat<Goal<Head : !second)
    (\$Threat<Goal<Head : !objective))

((\$rejection \$child-centred-decision -< >) **\$child-rejection**
    (\$Threat : non-residual)
    (\$Threat<Process : !go)
    (\$Threat : non-ranged))

((\$explanatory-cond \$logical-cond]-) **\$stated-cond**
    (\$Cond : unmarked-declarative-theme)
    (\$Cond : non-attitudinal))

((\$straight-threat
  \$explicit-repetition
 =}-) **\$repeat-straight**
    (\$Threat : thesis-repetitive))

((\$adult-centred-punishment
  \$chastisement
 -< >) **\$mother-punishes**
    (\$Threat : speaker-subject))

((\$adult-centred-punishment
  \$authority-figure
 -< >) **\$authority-punishes**
    (\$Threat : nominal-subject))

((\$child-centred-punishment
  \$authority-figure
 -< >) **\$punished-by-authority**
    (\$Threat : agentive))

(($child-centred-punishment
  $chastisement
  -<>) **$punished-by-mother**
    ($Threat : non-agentive))

(($punishment -[) **$smack**
    ($Threat<Process : !smack))

(($authority-figure -[) **$daddy**
    ($Threat<Actor<Head : !daddy)
    ($Threat<Actor : singular)
    ($Threat<Actor : non-determined)
    ($Threat<Actor : non-quantified))

((($rejection $command]-) $at-home =}-) **$threat-at-home**
    ($Threat<Spatial<Range : noun)
    ($Threat<Spatial<Range : singular)
    ($Threat<Spatial<Range : non-determined)
    ($Threat<Spatial<Range : non-quantified)
    ($Threat<Spatial<Range : non-possessive-nom)
    ($Threat<Spatial<Range<Head : !upstairs)
    ($Threat<Spatial : merged))

Notes

1. Halliday's work concerning the functional aspects of the language of young children reveals a larger number of less developed *macro-functions* (e.g. Halliday, 1978, pp. 50, 55-6, and especially 121). Note that the term *macro-function* in some of Halliday's earlier writings (e.g. 1973) and in Winograd (1983, p. 288) is also used to refer to what are now called *metafunctions*.

2. Since there is only one possible lexical item for the Subject, lexification has been used here. The following preselections would have the same result: Subject : singular,   Subject : personal,   Subject<Head : !second, Subject<Head : !subjective.

3. In fact, in this case *must* is <u>not</u> a modal, but rather what Halliday (1976c) calls a "quasi-modal" [!] or modulation (see also Halliday, 1985, p. 86). This is the difference between *Mary can't think that!* and *Mary can't think period!* (Halliday, 1976c). The former uses a modal to indicate that what is being said is obvious (the modal plays an interpersonal role); the latter uses a quasi-modal to indicate Mary's inability (the modulation plays an ideational role). Since the grammar used for the implementation cannot handle modulation, and since the syntax for the two is often identical, the current system pretends quasi-modals are true modals. This cheat prevents the implementation of the *$ubligation* examples such as *you'll have to go upstairs* since, unlike modulations, modals can never be combined with the future tense.

4. This proof is simplified by assuming that there is an "initial feature set" that contains not only those seeds which are given initially (as described in the discussion on generation), but also seeds which would be preselected during the generation. This does not affect the relevance of the proof because the origin of the seeds and the order in which they are added to the feature set is irrelevant.

5. Note the similarity between Nigel's grammar traversal and the "establish and refine" procedure described by Chandrasekaran et al. (e.g. 1984, pp. 24-5).

6. No doubt Winograd himself took advantage of the restricted field when constructing his grammar and lexicon, but his *program* did not.

Bibliography

D. E. Appelt, *Planning Natural-Language Utterances to Satisfy Multiple Goals*, Ph.D. thesis, Stanford University (1982). Also *Technical Note 259*, Stanford Reasearch Institute, Menlo Park.

———, "TELEGRAM: a Grammar Formalism for Language Planning," *Proceedings of the Eighth International Joint Conference on Artificial Intelligence*, pp. 595-9 (1983).

———, *Planning English Sentences*, (Cambridge University Press, Cambridge, U.K., 1985).

A. Barr, E. A. Feigenbaum, eds., *The Handbook of Artificial Intelligence*, Vol. I (Pitman, London, 1981).

R. Brachman, S. Amarel, C. Engelman, R. Engelmore, E. Feigenbaum, D. Wilkins "What are Expert Systems ?" in F. Hayes-Roth, D. Waterman, D. Lenat, eds., *Building Expert Systems*, pp. 31-58 (Addison-Wesley, London, 1983).

M. Brady, R. Berwick, eds., *Computational Models of Discourse* (M.I.T. Press, Cambridge, MA, 1983).

L. Brownston, R. Farrell, E. Kant, N. Martin, *Programming Expert Systems in OPS5* (Addison-Wesley, Menlo Park, 1985).

B. Buchanan, D. Barstow, R. Bechtal, J. Bennett, W. Clancey, C. Kulikowski, T. Mitchell, D. Waterman, "Constructing an Expert System," in F. Hayes-Roth, D. Waterman, D. Lenat, eds., *Building Expert Systems*, pp. 127-67 (Addison-Wesley, London, 1983).

A. Bundy, "AI 1 Problem Solving Notes," *Occasional Paper No. 30*, Department of Artificial Intelligence, University of Edinburgh (1983).

B. Chandrasekaran, S. Mittal, "Deep Versus Compiled Knowledge Approaches to Diagnostic Problem Solving," in M. Coombs, ed., *Developments in Expert Systems*, pp. 23-34 (Academic Press, London, 1984).

N. Chomsky, *Reflections on Language* (Fontana, Glasgow, 1975).

———, *Rules and Representations* (Blackwell, Oxford, 1980).

A. Davey, *Discourse Production* (Edinburgh University Press, Edinburgh, 1978).

W. Downes, *Language and Society* (Fontana, London, 1984).

J. R. Firth, "A Synopsis of Linguistic Theory (1930-1955)," in F. R. Palmer, ed., *Selected Papers of J. R. Firth 1952-1959*, pp. 168-205 (Longman, London, 1957).

C. L. Forgey, "OPS5 User's Manual," *CMU-CS-81-135* (Carnegie Mellon University, Pittsburgh, 1981).

J. Gaschnig, P. Klahr, H. Pople, E. Shortliffe, A. Terry, "Evaluation of Expert Systems: Issues and Case Studies," in F. Hayes-Roth, D. Waterman, D. Lenat, eds., *Building Expert Systems*, pp. 241-82 (Addison-Wesley, London, 1983).

B. Grosz, C. Sidner, "Discourse Structure and the Proper Treatment of Interruptions," *Proceedings of the Ninth International Joint Conference on Artificial Intellegence*, pp. 832-9 (1985).

M. A. K. Halliday, "Categories of the Theory of Grammar," *Word*, Vol. 17, pp. 241-92 (1961).

———, *Explorations in the Functions of Language* (Edward Arnold, London, 1973).

———, "Functions and Universals of Language," in G. Kress, ed., *Halliday: System and Function in Language*, pp. 26-31 (Oxford, London, 1976a).

———, "English System Networks," in G. Kress, ed., op. cit., pp. 101-35 (1976b).

———, "Modality and Modulation in English," in G. Kress, ed., op. cit., pp. 189-213 (1976c).

———, " Intonation and Meaning," in G. Kress, ed., op. cit., pp. 214-34 (1976d).

———, *Language as Social Semiotic* (Edward Arnold, London, 1978).

———, *An Introduction to Functional Grammar* (Edward Arnold, London, 1985).

M. A. K. Halliday, R. Hasan, *Cohesion in English* (Longman, London, 1976).

M. A. K. Halliday, J. R. Martin, eds., *Readings in Systemic Linguistics* (Batsford Academic, London, 1981).

D. Hasling, W. Clancey, G. Rennels, "Strategic Explanation for a Diagnostic Consultation System," in M. Coombs, ed., *Developments in Expert Systems*, pp. 117-33 (Academic Press, London, 1984).

F. Hayes-Roth, D. Waterman, D. Lenat, eds., *Building Expert Systems*, (Addison-Wesley, London, 1983).

———, "An Overview of Expert Systems," in ibid. pp. 3-29 (1983a).

L. Hjelmslev, *Prolegomena to a Theory of Language*, revised English edition, tr. Francis J. Whitfield (University of Wisconsin Press, Madison, 1961; original Danish version 1943).

J. Hobbs, "Granularity," *Proceedings of the Ninth International Joint Conference on Artificial Intelligence*, pp. 432-5 (1985).

J. Hopcroft, J. Ullman, *Formal Languages and their Relation to Automata* (Addison-Wesley, Reading, MA, 1969).

R. A. Hudson, *English Complex Sentences* (North-Holland, London, 1971).

———, "Systemic Generative Grammar," in M. A. K. Halliday, J. R. Martin, eds., *Readings in Systemic Linguistics*, pp. 190-217 (Batsford Academic, London, 1981).

A. deJoia, A. Stenton, *Terms in Systemic Linguistics* (Batsford Academic, London, 1980).

R. Kasper, "Systemic Grammar and Functional Unification Grammar," in J. Benson, W. Greaves, eds., *Proceedings of the 12th International Systemic Workshop* (Ablex, Norwood, N.J., 1987).

M. Kay, "Functional Unification Grammar," in *Proceedings of the Fifth Annual Meeting of the Berkeley Linguistics Society* (1979).

———, "Functional Unification Grammar: a Formalism for Machine Translation," in *Proceedings of COLING84*, pp. 75-8 (1984).

———, "Parsing in Functional Unification Grammar," in D. Dowty, L. Karttunen, A. Zwicky, *Natural Language Parsing*, pp. 251-78 (Cambridge University Press, London, 1985).

G. Kress, ed., *Halliday: System and Function in Language* (Oxford, London, 1976).

G. N. Leech, *Principles of Pragmatics* (Longman, London, 1983).

B. Malinowski, "The Problem of Meaning in Primitive Languages," supplement 1 to C. K. Ogden, I. A. Richards, eds., *The Meaning of Meaning* (Kegan Paul, London, 1923).

W. Mann, "The Anatomy of a Systemic Choice," *Discourse Processes*, Vol. 8, pp. 53-74 (1985).

W. Mann / M. A. K. Halliday, "Systemic Grammar of English, S. G. Clause Systems," from the PENMAN system, Information Sciences Institute, University of Southern California, Marina Del Rey [No date, but this is an early version].

W. Mann, C. Matthiessen, "Nigel: A Systemic Grammar for Text Generation," *RR-83-105*, Information Sciences Institute, University of Southern California, Marina Del Rey (1983).

M. P. Marcus, D. Hindle, M. M. Fleck, "D-Theory: Talking about Talking about Trees," in *Proceedings of the 21st Annual ACL Conference* (1983).

J. R. Martin, "Functional Components in a Grammar: a review of deployable recognition criteria," *Nottingham Linguistic Circular*, Vol. 13, special issue on systemic linguistics, pp. 35-71 (University of Nottingham, 1984).

M. McCord, "On the Form of a Systemic Grammar," *Journal of Linguistics*, Vol. 11, pp. 195-210 (1975).

D. D. McDonald, *Natural Language Production as a Process of Decision-Making under Constraints*, Ph.D. thesis, M.I.T. (Cambridge, MA, 1980).

———, "Natural Language Generation as a Computational Problem," in M. Brady, R. Berwick, eds., *Computational Models of Discourse* (M.I.T. Press, Cambridge, MA, 1983a).

———, "Description Directed Control: its implications for natural language generation," in N. Cercone, ed., *Computational Linguistics*, pp. 111-29 (Pergamon Press, Oxford, 1983b).

D. D. McDonald, J. Pustejovsky, "Description-Directed Natural Language Generation," *Proceedings of the Ninth International Joint Conference on Artificial Intellegence*, pp. 799-805 (1985).

K. McKeown, *Generating Natural Language Text in Response to Questions about Database Structure*, Ph.D. dissertation, University of Pennsylvania (1982).

———, "Focus Constraints on Language Generation," *Proceedings of the Eighth International Joint Conference on Artificial Intelligence*, pp. 582-9 (1983).

———, *Text Generation*, (Cambridge University Press, Cambridge, U.K., 1985).

E. Mishler, *The Discourse of Medicine* (Ablex, Norwood, New Jersey, 1984).

J. Monaghan, *The Neo-Firthian Tradition and its Contribution to General Linguistics* (Max Niemeyer Verlag, Tubingen, 1979).

N. Nilsson, *Problem-solving Methods in Artificial Intelligence* (McGraw-Hill, London, 1971).

T. Patten, "A Problem Solving Approach to Generating Text from Systemic Grammars," *Proceedings of the Second Conference of the European Chapter of the Association for Computational Linguistics*, pp. 251-7 (1985). Also *Research Report No. 260*, Dept. of Artificial Intelligence, University of Edinburgh.

———, *A Problem Solving Approach to Generating Text from Systemic Grammars*, Ph.D. thesis, University of Edinburgh (1986).

W. K. Purves, "A Biologist Looks at Cognitive AI," in *The AI Magazine* Vol. 6, pp. 38-43 (1985).

R. Quirk, S. Greenbaum, *A University Grammar of English* (Longman, Hong Kong, 1973).

R. Quirk, S. Greenbaum, G. Leech, J. Svartvik, *A Grammar of Contemporary English* (Longman, London, 1973).

G. D. Ritchie, *Computational Grammar* (Harvester, Sussex, 1980).

———, "Simulating a Turing Machine Using Functional Unification Grammar," *Proceedings of the European Conference on Artificial Intelligence* (1984).

———, "The Computational Complexity of Sentence Derivation in Functional Unification Grammar," *Proceedings of COLING-86* (1986).

E. Sacerdoti, "A Structure for Plans and Behaviour," *Technical Note 109*, Stanford Research Institute (Menlo Park, 1975).

B. C. Smith, "A Proposal for a Computational Model of Anatomical and Physiological Reasoning," *AI Memo 493*, M.I.T. (Cambridge, MA, 1978).

C. Sothcott, *EXPLAN: A System for Describing Plans in English*, M.Sc. dissertation, Dept. of Artificial Intelligence, University of Edinburgh (1985).

M. Stefik, J. Aikins, R. Balzer, J. Benoit, L. Birnbaum, F. Hayes-Roth, E. Sacer-
doti, "Basic Concepts for Building Expert Systems," in F. Hayes-Roth, D.
Waterman, D. Lenat, eds., *Building Expert Systems*, pp. 59-86 (Addison-
Wesley, London, 1983a).
———, "The Architecture of Expert Systems," in F. Hayes-Roth et al., eds., op.
cit., pp. 89-125 (1983b).
M. Sullivan, P. Cohen, "An Endorsement-Based Plan Recognition Program,"
*Proceedings of the Ninth International Joint Conference on Artificial Intel-
legence*, pp. 475-9 (1985).
A. Tate, "Interacting Goals and their Use," *Advance Papers of the Fourth Inter-
national Joint Conference on Artificial Intelligence*, pp. 215-8 (1975).
———, "Project Planning using a Hierarchic Non-linear Planner," *Reasearch
Memo No. 25*, Dept. of Artificial Intelligence, University of Edinburgh (1976).
H. Thompson, "Strategy and Tactics: A Model for Language Production," *Papers
from the Thirteenth Regional Meeting, Chicago Linguistics Society*, pp. 651-68
(1977).
R. Waltzman, *OPS5 Tutorial* (Teknowledge Inc., n.p., 1983).
D. Waterman, F. Hayes-Roth, "An Investigation of Tools for Building Expert
Systems," in F. Hayes-Roth, D. Waterman, D. Lenat, eds., *Building Expert
Systems*, pp. 169-215 (Addison-Wesley, London, 1983).
T. Winograd, *Understanding Natural Language* (Edinburgh University Press,
Edinburgh, 1972).
———, *Language as a Cognitive Process* (Addison-Wesley, London, 1983).
G. H. von Wright, *Explanation and Understanding* (Routlege Kegan Paul, Lon-
don, 1971).

Index

searching of, 119, 134
systemic syntactic structures, 5, **78-81**, 82, 86, 93-7, 102
see also syntactic structures
system label, 25, 113, 120
system network, 22, 24, **25-7**, 34, 44, 49, 72, **72**, 78, 82, 84, 78, 91, **99-102**, 153
LISP notation for, **111-15**, 116, 132

Tagfinite, 31
Tagsubject, 31
TELEGRAM, **140-2**, 149
teleology, 153
tenor, **46**, 47-50, 73, 154, 155
terminal nodes, 79, 80, 95, 99
terminal strings, 81, 86
terminal symbols, 78, 84, 85
TEXT, 133
text planning, 2, 64, 161, 178, 179, 181
Textual, 31, 69
textual metafunction, 39, 40, 41, 47, 48, 152
theory of computation, 147
Theme, 28, 31, 35, 36, 41, 58, 66, 69, 107, 127, 153
theme, 28, 31, 40
tone group, 32
Topical, 31, 34, 36, 57, 59, 66, 69, 70, 127, 128
transitivity, 27-30, 40
truth functions, 45
truth values, 97

Ullman, J., 79
unification, 140-1
unification grammar
see functional unification grammar
units, 33, 87, 96, 109, 128
unmarked features, 61, 152

valid feature sets, 85, 86, 87, 90, 91, 92, 94, 102
vectors, 126, 157, 159
Ventilator Manager, 11
verb network, 37, **190-2**

Waltzman, R., 126
Waterman, D., 13
well-formedness, 82, 86, 96, 97
Whorf, B., 19
Winograd, T., 24, 26, 28, 32, 34, 35, 37, 38, 39, 113, 140, 152, 155, 190, 192, 203
on the computational paradigm, 73-4

on functional linguistics, 23, 40
on systemic grammar, 22, 27
word rank, 36, 37, 44, 45, 71, 109, 161, 193
working memory, 6, 7, 8, 11, 106, 121, 123, 125, 127, 130, 132, 157-60
write, 128, 160